WALKS FOR ALL AGES
LEICESTERSHIRE & RUTLAND

WALKS FOR ALL AGES

LEICESTERSHIRE & RUTLAND

CLIVE BROWN

Published by Bradwell Books
9 Orgreave Close Sheffield S13 9NP
Email: books@bradwellbooks.co.uk

British Library Cataloguing in Publication Data: a catalogue record for this book is available from the British Library.

1st Edition

ISBN: 9781910551134

Print: CPI Group (UK) Ltd, Croydon CR0 4YY

Design by: Andy Caffrey

Typesetting and Mapping: Mark Titterton

Photograph Credits: Clive Brown, Allison Gilliver (p.14, p.80-81, p.84-85)
and credited individually. Front Cover image iStock

The information in this book has been produced in good faith and is intended as a general guide. Although the maps in this book are based on original Ordnance Survey mapping, walkers are always advised to use a detailed OS map. Look in 'The Basics' section for recommendations for the most suitable map for each of the walks
Bradwell Books and the authors have made all reasonable efforts to ensure that the details are correct at the time of publication. Bradwell Books and the authors cannot accept responsibility for any changes that have taken place subsequent to the book being published. It is the responsibility of individuals undertaking any of the walks listed in this book to exercise due care and consideration for their own health and wellbeing and that of others in their party. The walks in this book are not especially strenuous, but individuals taking part should ensure they are fit and well before setting off.
A good pair of walking books is essential for these walks. It is advisable to take good-quality waterproofs, and if undertaking the walks during the winter, take plenty of warm clothing as well. Because the walks will take some time, it would be a good idea to take along some food and drink.
Enjoy walking. Enjoy Leicestershire and Rutland with Bradwell Books!

CONTENTS

FOOTPATHS AND RIGHTS OF WAY IN LEICESTERSHIRE ARE POSSIBLY THE MOST COMPREHENSIVELY MARKED TRACKS IN THE COUNTRY. IT IS UNUSUAL IF A SIGNPOST DOES NOT MARK WHERE A FOOTPATH LEAVES A ROAD. IT IS PERHAPS MORE UNUSUAL IF A MARKER POST, WHICH HAS THE TOP 12 INCHES PAINTED YELLOW AND IS THEREFORE VERY EASILY SEEN, DOES NOT MARK A STILE OR OTHER SIGNIFICANT POINT WHERE A DECISION ABOUT DIRECTION NEEDS TO BE MADE. THE BOOK CONTAINS JUST A SMALL SELECTION OF WALKS WITHIN THE COUNTY; OTHER SUGGESTIONS ABOUT WHERE TO WALK INCLUDE BRADGATE PARK, WATERMEAD PARK, BEACON HILL AND SENCE VALLEY FOREST PARK.

Three Iron Age forts grace the skyline in Leicestershire; Burrough Hill, south of Melton Mowbray, Beacon Hill north of Leicester and Breedon on the Hill in the north-east of the county. The National Forest had its beginnings in the last years of the 20th century. Before the project started only 6 per cent of the area contained woodland. The company's aim is to increase the cover to 33,000 acres/135 square kilometres, particularly in locations that were once rural countryside that have been devastated by mining and excavation for quarries. The National Forest Way is a meandering 75-mile (120km) long trail, running from Beacon Hill Country Park in Leicestershire to the National Memorial Arboretum in Staffordshire.

Communications within the county benefit from some excellent infrastructure. The Midland Mainline Railway from Sheffield to St Pancras passes north–south through Leicester, crossed by the east–west Peterborough to Birmingham railway. The Roman road, Watling Street, now the A5, forms the south-western border between Leicestershire and Warwickshire. It used to be crossed close to Leicester by Fosse Way, running between Lincoln and Bath. Nowadays this route takes the Leicester western bypass and continues along the M69.

The county has more than its fair share of reservoirs, from the enormous Rutland Water down to the smaller drinking water reservoirs like Thornton, built during the middle of the Victorian era. Cropston and Swithland also supply drinking water, but the reservoir at Saddington provides water to keep the canal at the right level between Foxton and Leicester (see walk no. 19). All of the reservoirs are now havens for wildlife. Eyebrook has an interesting claim to fame; in 1943 it was used to represent the German reservoir and dam at Möhne, so that the crews of the 'Dambuster' Lancasters could practise before their historic bombing raid.

The city of Leicester's name appears to have derived from the Old English Caer Ligora or 'Castle on the Soar'. The Romans called their settlement Ratae, and it was the site of a bridge carrying the Fosse Way over the river. Leicester had been classed as a city with a bishop controlling a diocese in Saxon times, but lost this status during the struggle between Danes and Saxons. It did not become a city again until 1919 and a diocese and bishop were not restored until 1927 when St Martin's Church became a cathedral.

Stroll past a peaceful lake and a stately home that has royal connections.

The Baggrave Park estate used to be owned by Leicester Abbey and the villagers were moved on when the Abbey realised they could make more money from grazing sheep than allowing the local population to cultivate the land. Further up the hill from the hall are the humps and bumps in the grass marking the location of the deserted medieval village of Baggrave.

The present Hall in Baggrave Park dates from the late 17th century and it was built by John Edwyn on the site of an earlier building. The Edwyn line came to an end in 1770 when his daughter Anna married Andrew Burnaby; their grandson Edwyn Burnaby

was High Sheriff of Leicester in 1864. In 1881 Edwyn's granddaughter Cecilia (1862–1938) married Lord Glamis, who became the 14th Earl of Strathmore. Their daughter Elizabeth married the Duke of York in 1923, becoming Queen in 1936 and making the Burnabys ancestors of our present Queen.

During the latter part of the 20th century the hall, a listed building, was the subject of a planning dispute between the owners, a company run by the recently disgraced and jailed businessman Asil Nadir and the local planning authority, concerning unauthorised and unnecessary building work. The estate now has a new owner.

THE BASICS

Distance: 4½ miles / 7.25km

Gradient: Several easy slopes

Severity: Easy

Approx. time to walk: 2¼ hours

Stiles: Several stiles

Maps: OS Landranger 141 (Kettering & Corby); Explorer 233 (Leicester & Hinckley)

Path description: Grassy fields, good paths, a couple of sections of not very busy road, one short section of field that may be under cultivation and muddy, field edges and wider hardcore farm roads

Start point: The Golden Fleece, Main Street, South Croxton (GR SK 688102)

Parking: Sensible roadside parking in the village (LE7 3RL), limited bus service (check details)

Dog friendly: Several stiles, not easy for dogs

Public toilets: None

Nearest food: The Golden Fleece pub, Main Street, South Croxton

1. Go down Main Street towards the bridge and turn left at the footpath signpost, down the gravel drive to the gate on the right. Go through and walk down the right-hand edge of the lawn, follow the edge to the left, with the stream to the right, up to the stile at the yellow top marker post.

2. Step over and bear left to the stile at the trees, cross and go up the narrow enclosed path between hedges. The track bears right at the end, over a stile. Follow the field edge left and right, past a yellow top marker post to the yellow top marker post at the far corner. Take a right-hand diagonal (or the field edge right and left) to the stile at the trees.

3. Go over and keep on the obvious path through the trees, cross the stile at the far side and carry on to the fence ahead. Turn left, with the fence to your right, and keep right over the stile around the corner. Bear right and go through the gate at the hedge marked by a yellow top post.

4 Take the concrete farm road left, over the cattle grid and keep straight on along the road ahead. The road bears slight right. As it turns further right, go straight on through the narrow and then wide wooden gates. Continue up the wide grassy track between hedges and through the gate at the end.

5. Turn left, with the hedge to the left, downslope through two gates and bear right across the end of a field which may be under cultivation although a track should be well marked within any crop. Maintain direction along the left-hand field edge with the hedge to the left and go through the gate.

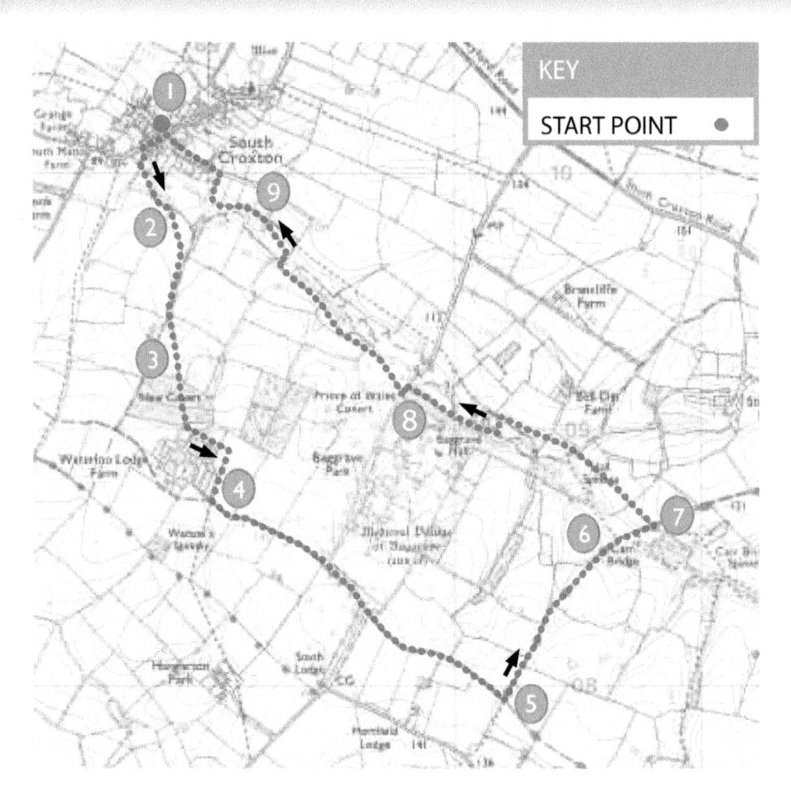

6. Bear right to the yellow top post at the dilapidated, brick-built Carr Bridge. Keep direction upslope through the gate with the hedge still left, to the stile on the left.

7. Go up the steps and across the stile, then keep ahead over the field and the stile. Carry on through the next boundary to the kissing gate ahead on the left in the corner. Go through and follow the path through the trees, over a footbridge and bear right with the lakes to the left. Carry on, passing right of Baggrave Hall, to the road.

8. Cross and continue through the kissing gate, next to the wide wooden gate at the far end and the kissing gate ahead. Go through both gates and over the footbridge at the far end; bear right through the wide gap and left with the hedge and the brook to the left. Keep ahead through the next kissing gate and along the path with the barbed-wire fence to the right.

9. Pass left of the pond and on through two more kissing gates, along the path through trees, bearing right to the narrow stony road. Turn left and carry on along the narrow tarmac road to the main road, passing right of the Golden Fleece to return to the start.

THE LEICESTER AND SWANNINGTON WAS ONE OF BRITAIN'S FIRST RAILWAYS, BORN OUT OF THE RIVALRY BETWEEN THE LEICESTERSHIRE AND NOTTINGHAMSHIRE COALFIELDS.

Rivalry had existed for years between the Nottinghamshire and Leicestershire coalfields in the early years of the Industrial Revolution to supply the developing town of Leicester. With both using horses and carts they could compete on equal terms, but the opening of the Erewash Canal and the Soar Navigation during the later years of the 18th century enabled Nottinghamshire coal to be transported to Leicester much more cheaply.

In the late 1820s local entrepreneurs John Ellis and William Stenson heard of the success of the new steam-operated railways and travelled to see the ground-breaking Liverpool and Manchester Railway then being built. They persuaded the railway pioneer George Stephenson to come to Swannington. His son Robert was the chief engineer of the railway and supervised the construction of the line. The Leicester and Swannington was built to a fairly primitive standard, where most of the track was level. There were, however, two slopes that contemporary locomotives could not negotiate. The Bagworth Incline, at 1 in 29, was self-acting; as the loaded wagons were lowered by cable from the top of slope, they hauled the empty ones back up as they travelled down.

The original route, opened fully in 1833, travelled through Glenfield Tunnel to a terminus at West Bridge in Leicester. The railway was quickly profitable, allowing coal to be sold much cheaper in Leicester and over a much wider area. Several more mines opened close to the line and the town of Coalville was established. The company was amazed to find that people wanted to travel on their trains; coaches were brought into service but were often just attached to the back of a coal train. Echoing modern health and safety fears, passengers had to get off the train at Bagworth and walk while the train negotiated the slope.

The line did not operate for very long under its original owners, and the directors sold out in 1845 to the acquisitive Midland Railway. The new owners soon had an easier route open between their station at London Road and the original line at Desford, avoiding the tunnel at Glenfield which would otherwise have needed widening. Deviations were also built around the two inclines with easier gradients to allow locomotive hauled-trains along the complete line.

Passenger trains have not used the railway since 1964; it has remained open for freight traffic only. Coal traffic ran until the 1980s when the local pits were all closed. Since then stone trains from Bardon Hill and Stud Farm Quarry near Markfield have been the line's only traffic.

Thornton Reservoir was opened in 1854 to supply water to Leicester, Hinckley and Nuneaton. Its surface area is 75 acres or 30 hectares and it holds 1.3 million square metres of water. A water treatment works was originally situated near the dam, but this process now takes place at the works attached to Cropston Reservoir. A 2½ mile/4km path leads right around the shoreline.

THE BASICS

Distance: 4¾ miles / 7.6km

Gradient: Several easy slopes

Severity: Easy

Approx. time to walk: 2½ hours

Stiles: Several stiles

Maps: OS Landranger 140 (Leicester); Explorer 245 (The National Forest) and 233 (Leicester and Hinckley)

Path description: Grassy fields and paths, fields which may be under cultivation and muddy, field edges and wider hardcore farm roads. A not very busy railway is crossed twice

Start point: Thornton Reservoir car park (GR SK 471075)

Parking: The car park at Thornton Reservoir (LE67 1AR). Bus service, check for details

Dog friendly: Several stiles, not easy for dogs

Public toilets: Next to the path around the reservoir a quarter of a mile from the car park

Nearest food: Refreshments at the building a quarter of a mile from the car park, next to the toilets. Pubs on Main Street, the Reservoir Inn and the Bricklayers Arms

1. Walk away from the car park to the left along the tarmac driveway with the reservoir to the right, past the toilet building, through the kissing gate and past the yellow-topped marker post. At the end, cross the bridge to the right and walk round to the kissing gate at the signpost. Go up the field edge to the first signpost.

2. Turn left, past the wide metal gate, along this wide, hedged track and keep ahead to the road. Turn left, down to the signpost on the right in the dip, step over the stile and the stile in the hedge left/ahead. Keep ahead, in a straight line across all the stiles to the road and turn left up to the corner and the signpost on the right.

3. Take the wide track to the right, between trees and bear left across a stile. Cross the field ahead, passing left of the pylon, to the yellow top post at the hedge. This field may be under cultivation but a track should be well marked within any crop. Carry on through the trees and the kissing gate, turn right to the marker post; go through the wide gap and ahead through the wooden kissing gates either side of the driveway.

4. Keep direction through two metal gates and up the wide, hedged track of Bagworth Incline for half a mile to the yellow top post on the left. Go over the stile and the stile on the right, cross the railway carefully and continue over the unusual concrete ladder stile to the field edge.

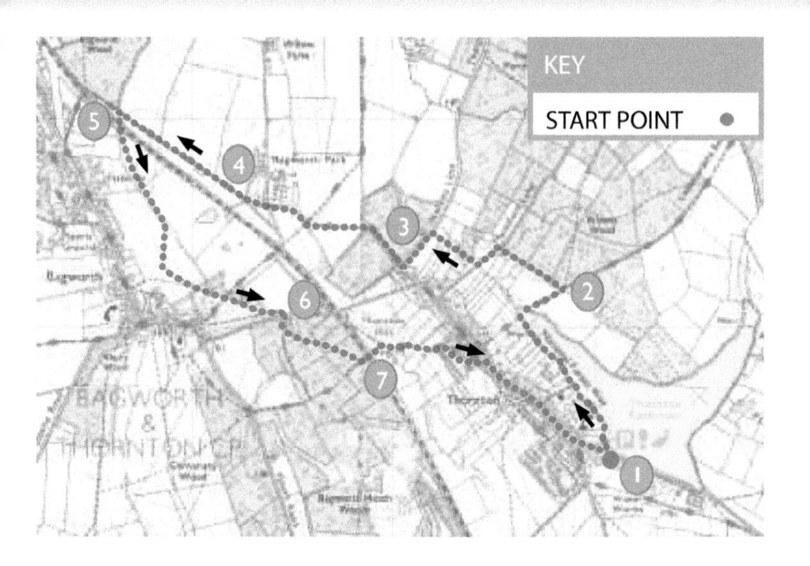

5. Follow the track signposted across the field which may be under cultivation, go through the hedge gap and turn left along the field edge with the hedge to the left, to the stile 50 yards right of the corner. Cross and bear left through the gap at the marker post, and carry on over the long footbridge in the dip and another footbridge in the narrow end of the field. Exit through the metal kissing gate on to the road.

6. Cross and take the path ahead at the signpost, bear left at the marker post and continue downslope, parallel with the telegraph poles, down to the railway.

7. Carefully cross back over the railway and the farm road, take the right-hand field edge ahead and go through the kissing gate. Keep ahead, over the footbridge and through the gates. Turn left up the driveway, passing right of the house, to the kissing gate on the right. Bear left through the kissing gate and go up the path to the left of the house. Turn right at the top and carry on ahead along Hawthorne Drive to Main Street. Take the roadside path right and turn left back down to the car park and the starting point.

Step back in time to Uppingham, which is evocative of a time when town centres all looked different.

So many country towns similar to Uppingham had heavily used trunk roads through their busy streets. The heavy traffic of the A47 between Leicester and Peterborough crossed the A6003 in the town centre. The bypass to the north was only completed in 1982.

Uppingham never had a very good railway connection in spite of the route between Kettering and Melton Mowbray passing only two and a half miles east of the town. A line running from Market Harborough to Peterborough also passes quite close along the

Welland Valley and a connection was eventually built from the village of Seaton on this line to Uppingham which opened in 1894. It was, however, never very successful, and closed to passengers in 1960, even before the Beeching cuts started.

A charter giving the town permission to hold the market which is still held each Friday was granted in 1281. Local historians believe that the market was already regularly held in the town and the charter was a merely a reaffirmation of the right, rather than a completely new idea.

The remains of a long-derelict medieval castle exist about a mile and a half north-east of Uppingham; it is believed to have been built during the civil war in the reign of King Stephen (1135–54).

Robert Johnson, a rich Tudor clergyman, who was an Archdeacon of Leicester and Rector of nearby North Luffenham, founded the schools in Uppingham and Oakham in 1584. Until the middle of the 19th century Uppingham remained quite a small school, educating up to sixty pupils at a time. The school expanded significantly to average over 300 during the headmastership of Edward Thring between 1853 and 1887. The school is now coeducational with a roll of around 800 pupils at a time. The school's original building still survives as a Grade I listed building and is part of the library complex.

THE BASICS

Distance: 2¾ miles / 4.5km

Gradient: Several easy slopes

Severity: Easy

Approx. time to walk: 1½ hours

Stiles: Two stiles and some gates

Maps: OS Landranger 141 (Kettering and Corby); Explorer 234 (Rutland Water)

Path description: Grassy fields, roadside paths, field edges and wider hardcore farm roads

Start point: In Uppingham town centre at the crossroads of High Street and Orange Street (GR SP 866996)

Parking: Car parks close by (pay and display) (LE15 9SQ). Good bus services

Dog friendly: Stiles difficult for dogs

Public toilets: In the centre of the town close to the start

Nearest food: A selection of pubs in the town of Uppingham

1. Go along Orange Street to the junction at the traffic lights and turn right along North Street East. Continue to the roundabout and keep ahead, on the road left of the thatched pavilion, cross the road and take the narrow tarmac drive, right/straight on.

2. As the driveway swings right follow the wide stony track ahead between hedges and carry on up the unfenced track between two fields. Keep direction through the trees and the track then driveway between hedges to the road in Bisbrooke. Turn left to the junction and right to the main road at the phone box.

3. Take the roadside path to the right to the footpath signpost on the right as the road swings left. Go up the wide track right/straight on, through the metal kissing gate and up the path ahead between the fence and the hedge.

4. Step over the stile in the hedge gap at the far end and continue up the field edge with the hedge to the left. The derelict railway viaduct can be seen to the left. Go over the next stile and bear slight right up the sharp slope in the sports field.

5. Exit through the wooden kissing gate to the road and turn right to the roundabout passed earlier. Take High Street East back to the starting point.

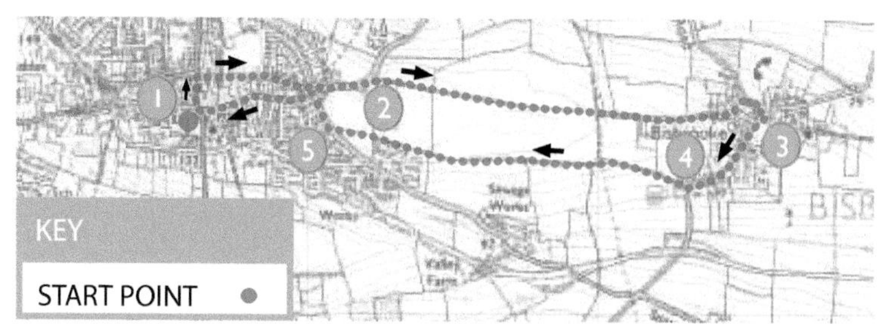
1
2
3
4
5
KEY
START POINT

ONE OF THE MOST IMPORTANT EVENTS IN ENGLISH HISTORY TOOK PLACE CLOSE TO HERE IN 1485, YET MODERN HISTORIANS CANNOT AGREE ON THE EXACT LOCATION OF THE BATTLE BETWEEN KING RICHARD III AND HENRY TUDOR. FOR SOME YEARS AMBION HILL, THE SITE OF THE BATTLEFIELD HERITAGE CENTRE AND COUNTRY PARK, WAS ACCEPTED AS THE POSITION BUT VARIOUS THEORIES NOW PLACE THE BATTLE AT UP TO A MILE AWAY.

The discovery of the remains of King Richard III under a car park in Leicester has reignited debate about his contribution to history. His controversial actions during his reign engender strong opinions, still likely to cause a robust argument over 500 years since his death.

Richard was born in Fotheringhay Castle on 2 October 1452. He was a staunch supporter of his brother King Edward IV, but the unexpected and early death of Edward on 9 April 1483 ended the settled peace that had held since the temporary cessation of the Wars of the Roses in 1471. Edward's elder son became Edward V, but as he was aged only 13 it was recognised that there would need to be someone looking after him. Richard, then Duke of Gloucester, was the obvious choice. The new king had been living in Ludlow; his maternal uncle Earl Rivers set out to bring him to London but was intercepted by Richard. Earl Rivers and some of his party were immediately arrested and executed soon after. Richard continued to London where he installed the young king in the Tower, which at the time was used as much as a palace as it was a fortress, and he was joined there soon after by his younger brother, also called Richard.

With a safe hold on the 'Princes in the Tower', Richard set out to secure his grip on power throughout England. During the early summer Richard removed more of his potential enemies and had them executed without trial. A story arose fuelled by various interested parties that Edward IVs marriage and therefore his children were illegitimate. Representatives of the people of London approached Richard and asked him to take the throne, which he did on 26 June after convincing Parliament, and had himself crowned ten days later.

The princes remained in the tower and were never seen again. It is unlikely that Richard was involved in the actual murder of the princes but it may have been done on his orders. Indeed it is not even certain they were murdered, as some historians now speculate that Edward may have died of natural causes. It is also possible that they were murdered by

someone trying to curry favour with Richard. There is also a strong belief among some people that the princes survived into the reign of Henry VII and were murdered on his orders as they would have been more of a threat to his kingship than Richard had been.

Richard faced the first revolt against him as early as the autumn of 1483. Nominally led by the Duke of Buckingham, who had been a staunch ally during the usurpation of the throne, the revolt was mainly supported by loyal followers of King Edward IV. Bad weather disrupted the rebel army and the same storm prevented an army led by Henry Tudor from landing in Devon. Buckingham was captured and beheaded.

It was another two years before the situation came to a head. Henry Tudor landed in South Wales with a small army in early August 1485 and marched through Wales gathering recruits and deserters from Richard's army.

Richard meanwhile gathered his forces at Leicester; his army reached there on 20 August, joining his ally the Duke of Norfolk. Further troops arrived on the 21st under the Earl of Northumberland. On the 22nd Richard's combined forces, thought to number about 10,000 men, occupied the top of Ambion Hill. A further army, nominally loyal to Richard and commanded by Baron Stanley and his brother William, was massed further away near Dadlington. Henry's forces are thought to have numbered only about 5,000. As the two armies met, Richard sent a message to Baron Stanley saying that if he did not attack immediately he would execute his son whom he was holding hostage. Stanley refused to react and replied that he had other sons. The son survived as his captors ignored Richard's orders to behead him, perhaps sensing the way things were going.

The fight went badly for the king in the first hand-to-hand fighting and he signalled for the Earl of Northumberland to attack, but his army remained stationary. Richard saw that Henry had ridden towards Stanley's position and he decided to engage him personally, leading a charge and coming to within a sword's length of Henry before he was stopped. The Stanleys joined in at this point on Henry's side and Richard was killed. The Duke of Norfolk had also been killed and Northumberland rode off with his army without taking part. The battle was over.

A legend perpetuated by the Shakespeare play tells of the finding of Richard's crown circlet worn on his helmet by Baron Stanley, who then crowned Henry on the battlefield. Richard's body was taken to Leicester and put on display before it was buried in Greyfriars Church. The church formed part of a monastery and was demolished during the reformation. Again facts about Richard are shrouded in mystery, as some people believed that his remains had been dug up and thrown into the River Soar. The car park now on the site of Greyfriars was the subject of an archaeological investigation during 2012 and a skeleton was found which proved to be that of the lost king. In March 2015 he was reburied with pomp and ceremony in the presence of royalty, in a splendid new tomb in Leicester Cathedral.

Shenton is the southern terminus of the Heritage Railway called the Battlefield Line, running through Market Bosworth to Shackerstone. The railway was promoted as the Ashby and Nuneaton Joint Railway and operated by the London and North Western Railway and the Midland Railway. It had been closed in the 1960s under the Beeching axe. Moves to preserve the line started in 1969, and the preservation society moved to Shackerstone in 1970. By the mid-1970s the line to Market Bosworth was in regular use and was extended to Shenton in 1992, when the first train was fittingly pulled by the tank locomotive ***Richard III***.

THE BASICS

Distance: 6 miles / 9.6km

Gradient: Several easy slopes

Severity: Easy

Approx. time to walk: 3 hours

Stiles: Quite a few

Maps: OS Landranger 140 (Leicester); Explorer 232 (Nuneaton & Tamworth)

Path description: Grassy fields, field edges, canal towpaths, wider hardcore farm roads, a section of not very busy road and a short stretch across a field which may be under cultivation and muddy if wet

Start point: The car park at Shenton Station (GR SK 396004). Or if starting from the Battlefield Heritage Centre (GR SK403001), pick up the walk from point 2 in the walk description

Parking: Shenton Station car park (CV13 6DP). It is also possible to park and start at the Bosworth Battlefield Heritage Centre car park (CV13 0AD); both pay and display

Dog friendly: Several stiles that are not good for dogs

Public toilets: In car park

Nearest food: Food and drinks when the station is open or there is a tearoom in Shenton village. Café at the Heritage Centre if starting there

1. Go to the yellow top marker post near the information board and cross the railway tracks (beware of trains on a working day). Bear left and immediate right, over the wide hardcore bridleway and keep ahead uphill, between the fence and the hedge. Follow the path right, to the monument.

2. Bear left downslope, passing right of the visitor centre, through two narrow metal gates and keep direction to the other side of Ambion Wood, bearing left with the canal to the right. Pass by the facilities at Sutton Wharf, go up to the road and turn right, over the bridge.

3. Turn right, down to the towpath and right, to follow the path with the canal now left. Carry on for two miles to Bridge no 27, opposite Stoke Golding. Turn right, over the marked stile and up to the right-hand end of the bridge.

4. Cross the road, go down the slope and over the narrow strip of field; cross the next stile/footbridge and turn left across the field which may be under cultivation, although a track should be well marked within any crop. Go past the yellow top marker post and keep direction; a track should still be visible and cross the stile footbridge in the gap.

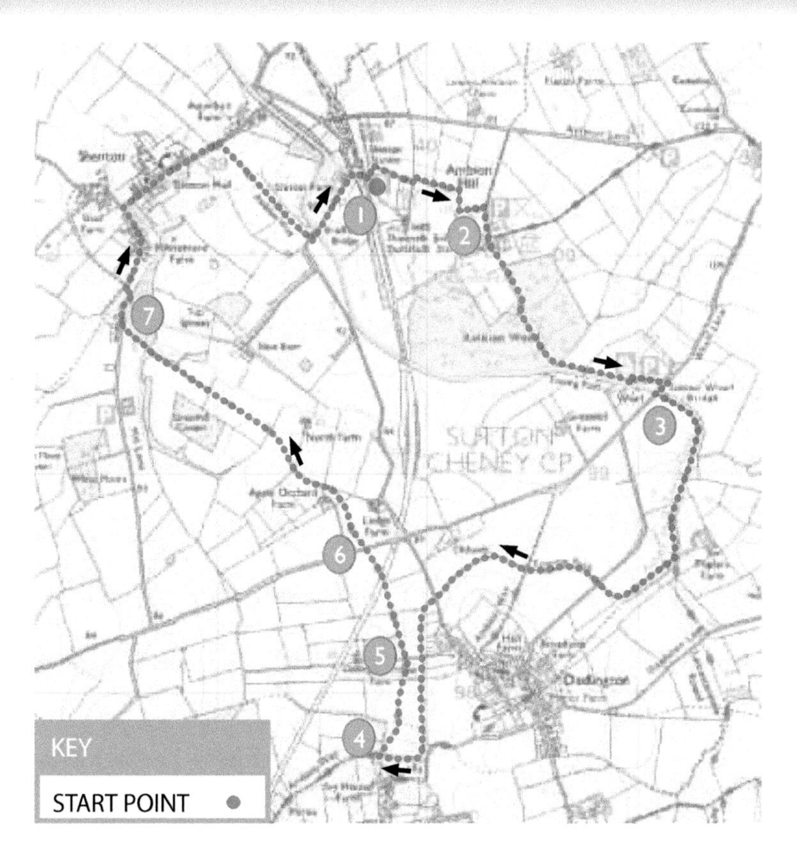

5. Carry on over the stiles either side of the farm road and up the left-hand field edge with the trees to the left. Keep ahead over the next two stiles and bear left over stiles either side of the disused railway embankment. Keep direction over stiles each side of the road.

6. Continue ahead through gaps marked by yellow top posts, passing right of Apple Orchard Farm. The track carries on slight left between the fence and the hedge. Step over the stile and bear right across the field; from the other side of the stile here the road keeps ahead through gates and over stiles to the road.

7. Turn right into Shenton village and follow the road left to the junction; turn right across the bridge over the stream. Carry on along Bosworth Road past the church and Shenton Hall to the footpath signpost on the right. Turn right, through the wide gate and keep straight on across the bridge all the way to the road. Take the road left over the humpback bridge across the canal to the car park on the right.

BRAUNSTON-IN-RUTLAND

BRAUNSTON WAS EASILY CONFUSED WITH ITS NAMESAKE IN NORTHAMPTONSHIRE AND EVEN MORE EASILY MISTAKEN FOR BRAUNSTONE, NOW A SUBURB OF LEICESTER, SO IT NOW USES THE IN-RUTLAND SUFFIX TO IDENTIFY ITSELF. LOOK OUT FOR THE EERIE STATUETTE!

The source of the River Gwash is close to the village of Knossington about three miles from Braunston-in-Rutland, but it only really becomes a river when joined by several more streams in the village area.

Braunston's church is dedicated to All Saints; paradoxically the church in the village of Braunston in Northamptonshire is also an All Saints. In the churchyard close to the tower is an enigmatic stone sculpture; it is a primitive carved figure with vaguely human features, a large mouth and prominent breasts. The carving has been made with a flat back and this is what has saved it for posterity; it was rediscovered in 1920, face down with the flat back in use as the doorstep into the church. No-one has been able to come up with a satisfactory explanation as to the purpose of the piece. It may even pre-date Christianity and the building of the church and been used in its construction as just another handy lump of stone.

The nearby town of Oakham is the county town of the historic county of Rutland. The town is thought to be Saxon in origin, possibly named after a prince or chieftain named Occa ('Occa's Homestead'). The name Rutland dates from the Domesday Book of 1086, but it is first mentioned as a separate county in 1159.

The great hall is the only remaining piece of Oakham Castle, which was built in the late 12th century as a fortified manor house. There is evidence that there was originally a moat, curtain wall and fortified towers. The building was in use until fairly modern times as a courthouse, and visitors during term time may find school parties re-enacting courtroom scenes. A continuing tradition at the castle rules that any peer of the realm visiting the town should present a horseshoe. This custom has gone on for at least 500 years, the earliest horseshoe dating from a visit by King Edward IV in about 1470. There are now over 200 specially made highly decorated horseshoes hanging upside down in the great hall. The upside-down horseshoe motif appears in the Rutland coat of arms. One of the latest horseshoes is not from a peer, but was presented by the TV host Michael Portillo on one of his 'Great Railway Journeys' through the town.

THE BASICS

Distance: 3¾ miles / 6km

Gradient: Several easy slopes

Severity: Easy

Approx. time to walk: 2 hours

Stiles: Two stiles and some gates

Maps: OS Landranger 141 (Kettering and Corby); Explorer 234 (Rutland Water)

Path description: Grassy fields, roadside paths, field edges and wider hardcore farm roads

Start point: All Saints Church, Church Street, Braunston-in-Rutland (GR SK 832065)

Parking: Sensible roadside parking in the village (LE15 8QT). Limited bus service (check for details)

Dog friendly: Stiles difficult for dogs

Public toilets: None on the route, try the pubs

Nearest food: The Old Plough, Church Street or the Blue Ball, Cedar Street, Braunston-in-Rutland

BRAUNSTON-IN-RUTLAND WALK

1. Go into the churchyard, along the path past the church porch and doorway. Continue through the narrow wooden gate and the kissing gate/footbridge. Bear left across the field, through the wide hedge gap and the footbridge here.

2. Keep ahead along the faint track in the grass, over the footbridge/stile and maintain direction with the hedge to the right (the track should still be showing in the grass), and step over the stile on the right. Turn left, along the field edge with the dyke and the hedge to the left, over the single plank footbridge in the corner and carry on with the hedge still left. Go past the yellow top marker post and up the slight slope to the wide farm track at the top.

3. Turn right, follow the track left then right and cross the footbridge in the hedge gap. Bear right, on a less well-used track to a junction; bear right past a yellow top marker post, over a footbridge and along a track through trees. Keep ahead on the better path and join the track straight on in the clearing. Turn right past two marker posts in a hedge gap and keep on this track passing right of a pond, through a gate and over a footbridge on to a wide grassy track.

4. Take this track right, with the trees of the wood called Top Windmill to the left and carry on to the narrow metal gate. Turn left, then right, through the narrow wooden gate slightly further on than the wide metal gate. Turn sharp right along another wide bridleway between hedges to the point where the track swings left at opposite gateways (before the wide metal gate).

5. Turn right, into the field, downslope right of the faint track in the grass, to the far side hedge, where a stile can be difficult to find in the trees of the boundary. Cross and bear left to the far, bottom corner (marked by a yellow top post) and cross this stile; carry on along the left-hand field edge into the next corner and go over the footbridge/stile. Turn right, along the right-hand field edge, passing right of South Lodge Farm.

6. Continue up the wide track, through the kissing gate, a metal gate and over the sturdy, sleeper-based footbridge. Carry on up the field edge with the trees to the right, through the wide gap in the boundary and up to the stile on the right. Cross and keep ahead down this hedged path, then bear slight right over the stile/footbridge at the end. Keep direction with the hedge to the left, over the stile/footbridge in the next corner. Carry on to the gates this side of the church at the beginning of the walk and retrace your steps into the churchyard.

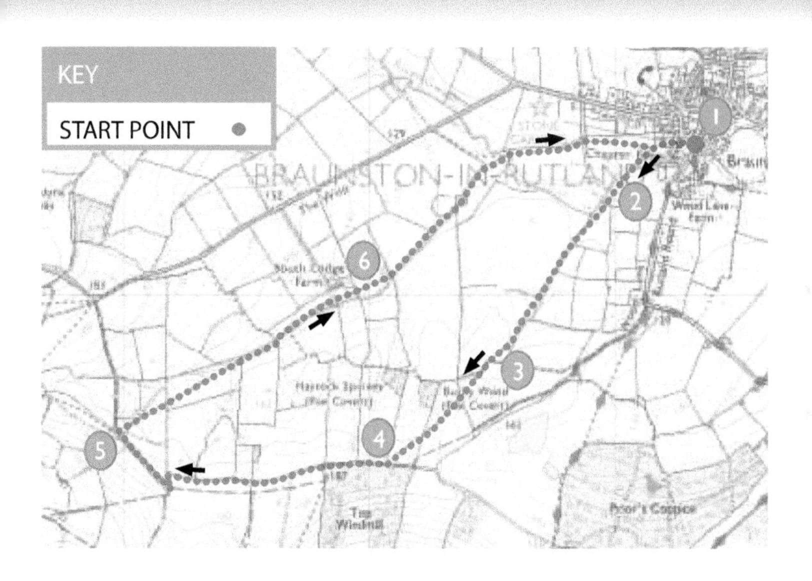
KEY
START POINT
BRAUNSTON-IN-RUTLAND
1
2
3
4
5
6

BURBAGE COMMON

BURBAGE IS AN OBSCURE SUBURB OF THE SMALL TOWN OF HINCKLEY, ON THE WESTERN EDGE OF LEICESTERSHIRE. IT IS A PLEASANT SURPRISE TO FIND SUCH A DELIGHTFUL OPEN SPACE, ASSOCIATED WOODLAND AND A NATURE RESERVE JUST OUTSIDE THE TOWN. THE AREA IS HOME TO OR VISITED BY OVER 100 SPECIES OF BIRDS AND A WIDE VARIETY OF INSECTS AND PLANTS.

Hinckley is listed in the Domesday Book as having a value of £4; it had only forty years earlier been valued at just two shillings when it was given to the Abbey at Coventry by Leofric, the Earl of Mercia. He is better remembered in history as the husband of Lady Godiva.

The railway line passing through the common on an embankment is the line running between Leicester and Birmingham via Nuneaton. It has narrowly avoided closure several times but now forms an important link between Birmingham and East Anglia, by way of Peterborough and Cambridge. The line was originally built and owned by the London and North Western Railway, opening in 1847. The A47 trunk road from the centre of Birmingham which continues east to Great Yarmouth also once ran through the town centre. The bypass running north of the town was opened in 1994.

The de Montfort family, Earls of Leicester during the early Middle Ages, held property at Shilton, east of Burbage and Hinckley. The 5th Earl had land enclosed and stocked with game to create a park so that he and his guests could amuse themselves hunting and providing meat for their table. The town became known as Earl Shilton through its association with him. His son, also Simon, the 6th Earl, played a much greater part in English history; he led the revolt in 1265 against King Henry III that resulted in the first directly elected Parliament. He effectively ran the country in the name of the King until his defeat and death at the Battle of Evesham the next year.

THE BASICS

Distance: 2¾ miles / 4.5km

Gradient: Flat

Severity: Easy

Approx. time to walk: 1½ hours

Stiles: None

Maps: OS Landranger 140 (Leicester); Explorer 233 (Leicester & Hinckley)

Path description: Grassland, hard driveways and good paths

Start point: Car park at Burbage Common (GR SP 446953)

Parking: Car park at Burbage Common (LE10 3DD)

Dog friendly: Yes

Public toilets: At the visitor centre

Nearest food: Acorns Coffee Shop at the visitor centre

1. Take the track in the grass away from the car park between the visitor centre and Burbage Common Road, bearing right, away from the road. Keeping direction along the wide grassy area, continue beneath the railway bridge.

2. Keep straight on/left along the narrow hardcore track, through the car park and along the entrance road, then follow the road right.

3. As the road swings slight left, turn right, through the roomy kissing gate, past the 'Welcome to Burbage Wood' sign and bear left on a slightly narrower path winding through the trees bearing right. Turn left with the edge of the trees to the far left corner.

4. Turn sharp right, keeping to the edge of the trees, and at the junction of paths at the next corner take the track to the right, a little further into the trees. The path swings left to another entry point and carries on along the edge. Cross the footbridge at the end and turn immediately left, through a wooden kissing gate.

5. Carry on along the field edge, with the trees and hedge to the left, through the kissing gate near the railway. Continue along the hardcore farm road and turn right, back under the railway line. Keep ahead along the edge of the wood with the stream to the left past the signpost and carry on all the way to the green kissing gate. Go through and bear right, back to the visitor centre and the car park.

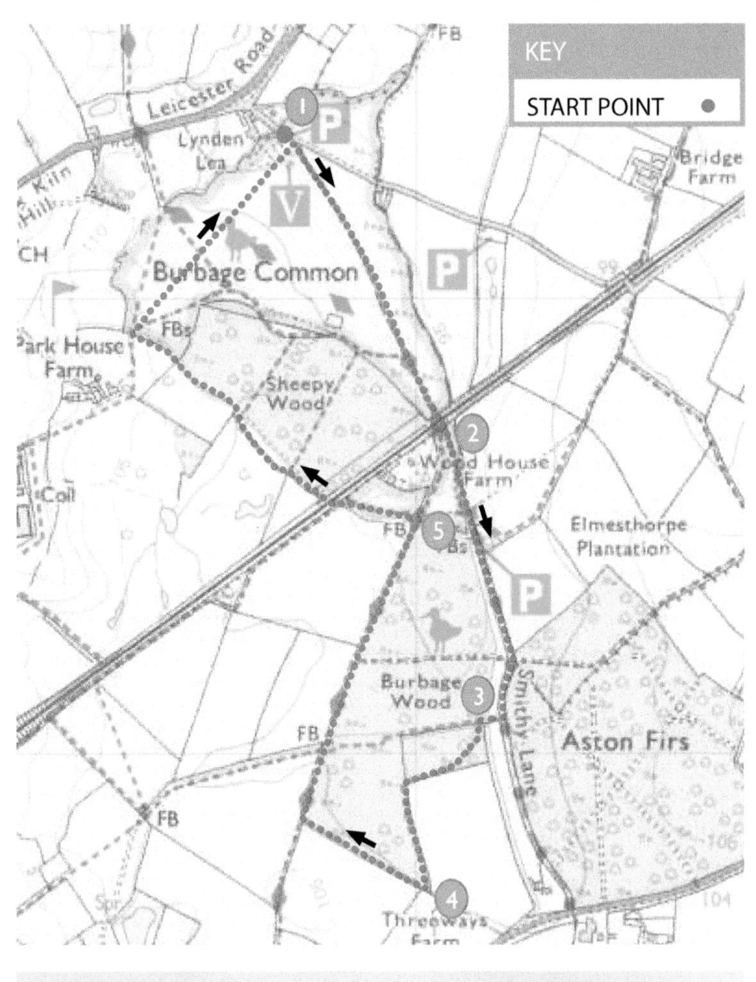

Mat Fascione

BURROUGH HILL FORT

THE IRON AGE COVERED APPROXIMATELY THE MILLENNIUM BEFORE THE ARRIVAL OF THE ROMANS. THE RESIDENTS OF THIS COUNTRY LIVED MAINLY IN SMALL VILLAGE SETTLEMENTS UNTIL ABOUT 700 BCE, WHEN FOR A VARIETY OF REASONS THEY STARTED TO LIVE IN FORTS DUG INTO THE TOPS OF HILLS.

The 660ft/200m high fort at Burrough Hill is believed to have been built and occupied from about 500 BCE. It continued to be occupied into the Roman Era. The hill is possibly the main settlement of the Coritani, the dominant British tribe in the area before the arrival of the Romans.

There have been major archaeological digs throughout the 20th century, yielding a great deal of knowledge about historic Leicestershire and its early inhabitants. An investigation has been digging on the hill since 2010. An important find towards the end of 2014 was the bronze fittings of a sophisticated chariot, which would have been suitable for a chief or some other important member of the tribe. Historians have so far been unable to decide how the remains came to be buried. It is quite possible that the chariot was burned and the ashes and fittings buried, or perhaps the fittings were just buried to make the building of the vehicle much easier in the afterlife. There is evidence that the inhabitants lived in roundhouses made of stone or earth walls with a cone-shaped thatched roof of the type built experimentally at several museums of Iron Age culture.

Burrough Hill was under cultivation in the Middle Ages with some remaining ridge and furrow systems to be seen. This was created by a traditional plough which would turn the soil only one way, and as the plough went backwards and forwards over narrow strips of land it piled the soil into the centre of the strip, leading to a slope up to a ridge one way and down into the furrow on the other. It is believed that the fort was used as a location for a fair every Whit Monday, including various sporting events and ending with dancing.

During the 19th century horses were raced inside the fort, transforming it into a medieval amphitheatre where the spectators used the earth ramparts as grandstands. In the last years of the 20th century a horse called Burrough Hill Lad, named after the equine association, had some success on the National Hunt racing scene, winning three of the major races including the Cheltenham Gold Cup during the 1984 season.

THE BASICS

Distance: 3 miles / 4.8km

Gradient: One stiff slope

Severity: Moderate

Approx. time to walk: 1½ hours

Stiles: None

Maps: OS Landranger 129 (Nottingham & Loughborough, right on the edge); Explorer 246 (Loughborough)

Path description: Grassland, good paths, a section of not very busy road and a short length of field which may be under cultivation and could be muddy

Start point: The car park at Burrough Hill Country Park (GR SK 766115)

Parking: The car park at the Country Park (Pay and display; exact money needed) (LE14 2QZ). Limited bus service (check details)

Dog friendly: Yes

Public toilets: At the car park

Nearest food: Grant's Free House, Main Street, Burrough on the Hill

BURROUGH HILL FORT WALK

1. Walk away from the road through the kissing gate at the wide wooden gate and continue down the hardcore road, right of the farmyard to the wide wooden gate just past the information board.

2. Go through and take the path bearing left through a gap, downhill with the fort ramparts sloping up to the right. Continue down the narrower track through the gorse and then with the hedge to the left. Go through the gates at the bottom, marked by a yellow top post, to the slight right. Follow the field edge right and left, down to the road.

3. Turn right and keep straight on/right at the junction, up to Moscow Farm at the corner. Take the farm road ahead, to the signpost on the right.

4. Turn right over the stile, walk downslope to the marker post and cross the bridge between fields. Cross the field ahead, which may be under cultivation, although a path should be well marked within any crop. Pass left of the stunted tree to the yellow top marker post in the hedge ahead.

5. Go through the gate and turn left for 30 yards to the signpost, step over the stile and take the right-hand field edge bearing left with the hedge to the right. Carry on upslope through the trees, joining the wider track right/straight on, through the wide wooden double gates. Keep ahead past a yellow top post, upslope bearing right, past two more marker posts and carry on over the ridge and furrow field. Go through the entry gate at the information board and turn left back to the car park.

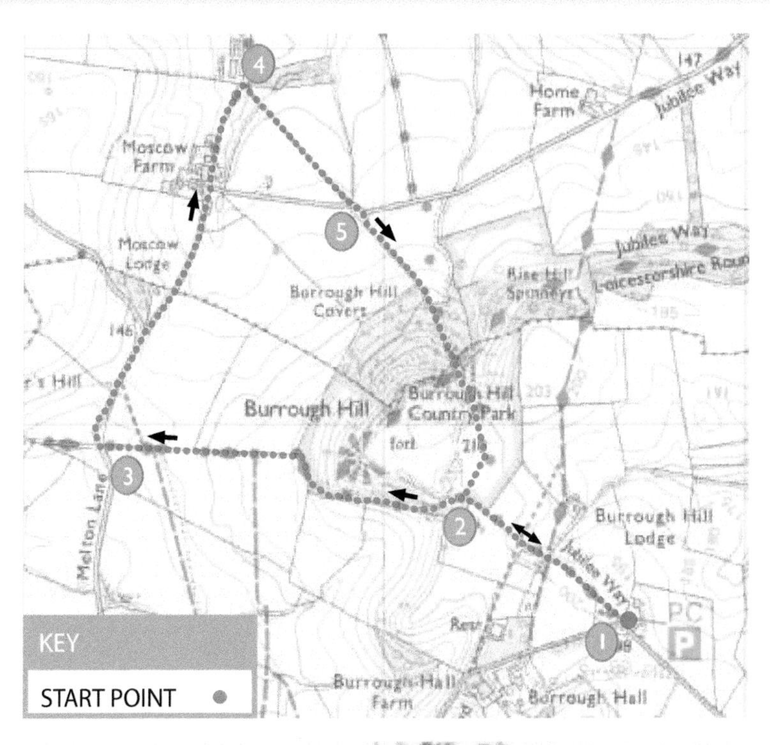

Moscow Farm
Moscow Lodge
Home Farm
Jubilee Way
Burrough Hill Covert
Rise Hill Spinney
Leicestershire Round
Burrough Hill
Burrough Hill Country Park
fort
Melton Lane
Burrough Hill Lodge
Burrough Hall Farm
Burrough Hall
KEY
START POINT

COSSINGTON MEADOWS

AT 187 ACRES (75 HECTARES), COSSINGTON MEADOWS IS THE LARGEST NATURE RESERVE IN THE SOAR VALLEY. IT IS A FORMER GRAVEL PIT OPERATIONAL DURING THE 1980S AND 90S; THE SITE WAS ACQUIRED BY THE LEICESTERSHIRE AND RUTLAND WILDLIFE TRUST IN 2004.

A certain amount of land reclamation has been carried out; the deeper pits have been filled with bricks and other suitable materials. Topsoil has been laid and seeded with grass; flooding will be allowed to take place naturally to form shallow muddy pools to encourage wading birds. Floodwater will also bring in suitable seeds to augment the resident range of wetland plants. The reserve is already home to or regularly visited by a wide assortment of birds, wildflowers and plants.

The River Soar south of Cossington close to Junction Lock is joined by one of its larger tributaries, the River Wreake. The source of the river is close to Stapleford, east of Oakham, and between here and Melton Mowbray it is known as the River Eye. The river between Melton Mowbray and the confluence with the Soar was rebuilt into a canal or 'navigation' completed in 1797. This connected the town with the Soar Navigation and the rest of the country's canals. A separate company opened the Oakham Navigation in 1802. The Oakham Canal never really succeeded financially and when the Syston to Peterborough Railway was planned, the company bought the canal and used some sections of its route. The Melton Canal never prospered after the railway's arrival and closed in 1877.

THE BASICS

Distance: 2¾ miles / 4.5km

Gradient: Flat

Severity: Easy

Approx. time to walk: 1½ hours

Stiles: None

Maps: OS Landranger 129 (Nottingham & Loughborough); Explorer 246 (Loughborough)

Path description: Grassland, good paths, field edges and riverbank

Start point: All Saints Church, Cossington (GR SK 604136)

Parking: The car park as above (LE7 4UU). Limited bus service (check details).

Dog friendly: Yes

Public toilets: None

Nearest food: The Royal Oak, Main Street, Cossington

1. Go through the kissing gate in the fence and bear left through the kissing gate at the yellow top marker post in the fence on the left.

2. Turn immediate right, past a second yellow top marker post, along the path between trees and a dyke; go through this kissing gate and past the Cossington Meadows signboard. Keep ahead along the obvious track to a yellow top marker post and turn left to the post next to a wide metal gate.

3. Turn left on this wide vehicle track between hedges to the end and go through the two kissing gates to the road.

4. Cross and step over the stile opposite, then bear right up the field over the stile at the far left. Go up the steps to the road and turn left, through the narrow metal gate at the end to a yellow top post. Turn right, over the footbridge on the path through the trees, turn right and follow the track left, through the kissing gate and along the field to the end of the substantial footbridge.

5. Continue ahead with the river to the right, all the way to Junction Lock. Just past the lock where there is a fence on right, turn left on the path over a small humpback bridge.

6. Take the track left, then right, with the lake to the left and follow the path right, between trees to the road. Cross carefully to Platts Lane ahead and take the roadside path bearing right to a kissing gate opposite the sports field.

7. Turn left through this kissing gate into Cossington Meadows. Bear right, through the kissing gate at the far right; continue right of the lake, through a kissing gate again at the far right. Take the path through the trees with the moat now right, through the gate and over the footbridge to the yellow top marker post at the kissing gate ahead. Go through and bear right back to the car park and starting point.

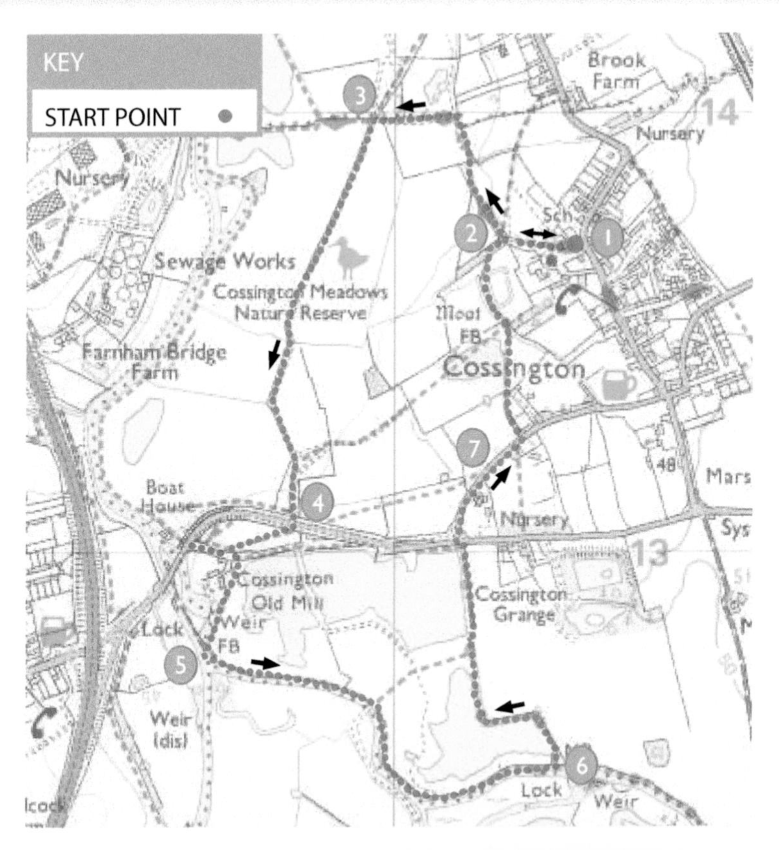
KEY
START POINT
Brook Farm
Nursery
Sch
Nursery
Sewage Works
Cossington Meadows Nature Reserve
Moat
FB
Farnham Bridge Farm
Cossington
Boat House
Nursery
Cossington Old Mill
Weir
FB
Lock
Cossington Grange
Weir (dis)
Lock
Weir

CROSS A BLEAK MAN-MADE LANDSCAPE AND DISCOVER A FAIRYTALE CASTLE HIDDEN AWAY IN TREES. RETURN THROUGH TWO PLEASANT VALLEYS TO THE SOUND OF BABBLING BROOKS. EXTON IS A REALLY OLD-FASHIONED PICTURESQUE VILLAGE CONCEALED FROM MAJOR ROADS.

Sir Baptist Hicks purchased the Exton Park estate in 1613, after it had previously been owned by Sir John Harrington who had been bankrupted by the expense of looking after Princess Elizabeth, the daughter of King James I. The avenue of trees leading into the estate is still called the 'Queen of Bohemia's Ride'. Elizabeth is remembered in history as the 'Winter Queen'; her grandson nevertheless became George I, Britain's first Hanoverian King.

Hicks became Viscount Campden but died without a male heir; his daughter Juliana married Sir Edward Noel, who became the 2nd Viscount. The wonderfully named Baptist Noel, the 3rd Viscount, took the royalist side in the Civil War and the estate was forfeited until the Restoration. His son Edward became the first Earl of Gainsborough in 1682.

The lakes in Exton Park were constructed in the early 18th century. Fort Henry was built on the side of the Upper Lake in the 1780s for the family to entertain guests as a superior form of summerhouse. The Old Hall burnt down in 1810 and a farmhouse was used as the residence in the interim. In 1850 the house was rebuilt much larger and this remains as the Gainsborough Stately Home.

In 1948 the United Steel Company leased an area of the park to enable them to quarry ironstone. The area between the lakes and the village, crossed at the first part of the walk, was quarried until 1974. The ore was taken away by an industrial railway, through the site of the 'Rocks by Rail' museum near Cottesmore to the mainline railway at Ashwell

Junction. The site was the first home of the giant dragline, ***Sundew*** (named after the 1957 Grand National winner). This massive machine weighed 1,675 tons and had to be brought to the quarry in pieces and assembled on site. It had a jib 282ft/86m long and the capacity of its bucket was 27 tons, with a corresponding work rate of 1,600 tons per hour. When the quarry closed in 1974 it was decided to relocate ***Sundew*** to a quarry near Corby. Dismantling and reassembly was considered but this was not economically viable. To move anywhere the dragline had huge feet which were put down to the ground while the machine shuffled forward, something like a baby moving around on its bottom. It was decided to walk the machine to its new place of work; in a highly planned operation it walked for 13 miles across country, over a river, a railway line and ten roads including the A43 and the A47. Sundew carried a banner on its back saying 'EXCUSE ME! I'm walking to Corby'. The journey took nine weeks at a speed when moving of a mile every ten hours and cost a quarter of a million pounds.

By 1980 the quarry had been closed and ***Sundew*** was laid up while its owners considered their options. In 1987, looking very forlorn and with vegetation almost obscuring it, the scrap dealers moved in and cut it up; this in itself took six months. Only the cab survives at 'Rocks by Rail'; the museum has recently received a grant from the Lottery Fund to renovate it.

THE BASICS

Distance: 4¾ miles / 7.6km

Gradient: Some moderate slopes

Severity: Easy

Approx. time to walk: 2¼ hours

Stiles: Several stiles

Maps: OS Landranger 130 (Grantham, right on the edge); Explorer 234 (Rutland Water)

Path description: Substantial estate roads, good paths, grassland and field edges

Start point: The village green at the centre of Exton (GR SK 926113)

Parking: Sensible roadside parking (LE15 8BY). Limited bus service (check details).

Dog friendly: Several stiles restricting dog access

Public toilets: None

Nearest food: The Fox and Hounds pub in the village. Nearby pubs are the White Horse in Empingham, the Noel Arms in Whitwell and the Sun Inn in Cottesmore

EXTON PARK WALK

1. Take New Field Road away from Stamford Road, over the cattle grid and along the rough tarmac estate road, bearing left with the iron railings made from old rails to the right. Follow the road downslope to a T-junction/crossroads at a signpost.

2. Keep straight on, upslope on the grassy track ahead, over the summit and continue ahead/right along a tarmac driveway passing between the two lakes. Walk up the slight slope to the signpost on the left and turn left along the field edge for 250 yards to get a good view of Fort Henry on the other shore of the lake. Return to the road and turn right, back to the signpost on the left.

3. Step over the stile and take the track in the grass ahead, with Lower Lake to the right, past a wide metal gate to a three-way signpost. Keep straight on along the slope of the valley to a stile marked by a yellow top post and cross and continue your direction with the hedge and telegraph poles to the left. Bear right, with the line of telegraph poles across the concrete bridge over North Brook; go through the gate and walk along the left-hand field edge, with the fence to the left, bearing right to the road.

4. Turn right and follow the road left, to the signpost on the right; turn right, through the hedge gap and on to the hedge ahead. Turn left along the field edge with the hedge to the right for 25 yards and turn right, over the stile. Cross and bear left downslope, over the footbridge at the yellow top marker post.

5. Take the field edge left, with the fence and the stream to the left, upslope to the corner. Turn left into the trees, descend the boardwalk and cross the footbridge.

6. Turn right along the track with the stream now right for 300 yards and cross back over the stream. Turn left, back to the original direction with the stream again left. Follow the track as it bears right upslope through a wide hedge gap and carry on with the hedge to the right, to a T-junction of tracks at the trees.

7. Turn right, with these trees to the left, and turn immediate left, along the field edge with the hedge and the trees to the left, upslope. Take the track left with the hedge to the right, up to a signpost and turn left on the wider track past a metal gate. Keep direction along Garden Road to Stamford Road, back to the junction with New Field Road.

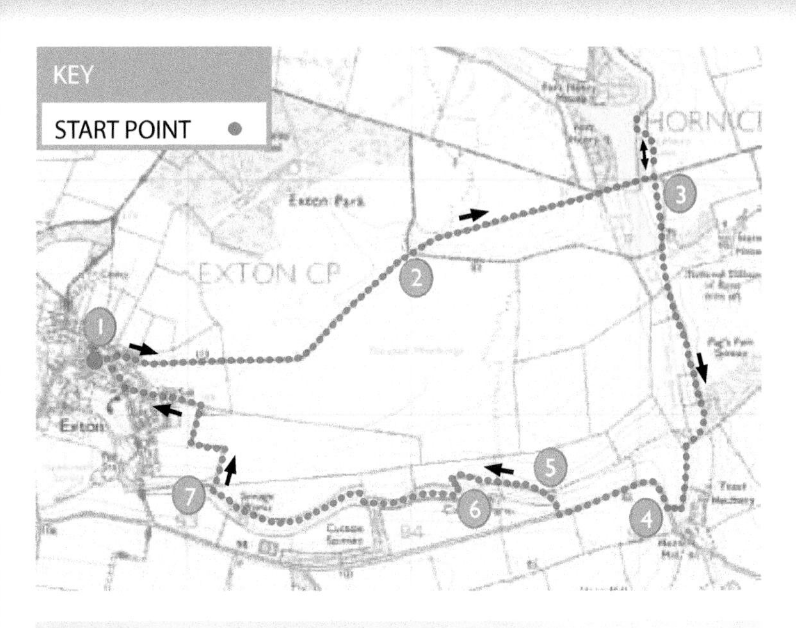
KEY
START POINT
EXTON CP
Exton Park
Exton
1
2
3
4
5
6
7

A RAILWAY LINE THAT IS MUCH MORE EFFECTIVE FOR PEOPLE WALKING THAN IT EVER WAS FOR TRAIN PASSENGERS. THE LINE WOULD POSSIBLY BE FAR MORE SUCCESSFUL THESE DAYS IF IT WERE STILL OPEN. BE WARY OF FAST-MOVING CYCLISTS, AS THE ROUTE IS NOW BOTH A FOOTPATH AND A BUSY CYCLEWAY.

Like so much of the butchery of the railway system during the sixties, closing the Great Central main line is widely believed to have been a mistake. The Manchester, Sheffield and Lincolnshire Railway (MSLR) was formed in 1847 from a merger of a series of smaller railways within these areas. It was the biggest of the Victorian railways not to have its own main line into a London terminus and always coveted one.

Edward Watkin had been the General Manager of the MSLR and became its chairman in 1864; he started to push for the railway to build its 'London Extension' and had a grand design for a railway line running all the way from Manchester to Paris. He was also chairman of the Metropolitan Railway (through London) and the South Eastern Railway (between London and Dover) and a director of the French Chemin de Fer du Nord (Calais to Paris). He had also been behind a company that started to construct a Channel Tunnel in 1880. Various Victorian politicians, dignitaries and royalty did not like the idea. Many of them believed it would make a French invasion easier.

The tunnel had actually progressed more than a mile and a quarter towards its destination when Parliament ordered that it had to be stopped. Watkin continued to push for a mainline London Extension and finally got a Parliamentary Bill passed in 1893 authorising the railway. The route was the only one of the major lines not built with spades, picks and wheelbarrows. Technology had advanced so much since the construction of the earlier lines that the contractors were able to use steam-powered excavators and other more modern equipment. The line was built to a very high standard so that trains could travel at a sustained and comfortable high speed, and a great deal of thought was given to making the stations easier to use and passenger friendly.

In order to reflect its new national status the company changed its name in 1897, becoming the Great Central Railway. The new route ran through Nottingham from Annesley and continued through Loughborough, Leicester and Rugby; south of the industrial Midlands it ran through areas of low population and was never as successful as hoped. The company became part of the London and North Eastern Railway and then British Railways in 1948, and the line was always regarded as the poor relation of the other north–south main lines.

When traffic stared to decline with the onset of wider car ownership and the success of road transport in the 1950s and 60s, other lines started to close. The Beeching axe started to swing; the Great Central main line was the subject of constant speculation in the railway press and periodicals as to when it would close completely. Through trains from Nottingham to London ceased in 1960 and the route became more and more run down, finally closing between Nottingham and North London in 1969.

There are two preserved railway organisations currently using the line: the Great Central Railway, based in Loughborough, running trains south to Leicester North; and the Nottingham Transport Heritage Centre based at Rushcliffe Country Park, who operate trains to the south towards Loughborough. Long-term plans aim to join these railways and operate a double track for 18 miles between Ruddington and Leicester. This project has to overcome major civil engineering problems because the infrastructure was all removed when the line closed.

The route of the dismantled railway was adapted during the 1980s into a four-mile long path and cycleway. It runs from Braunstone Gate to Glen Parva. The path has created a wildlife corridor packed with birds, small animals and insects. The path is extensively used by commuters, joggers, dog walkers, nature lovers and mothers with pushchairs. In an echo of Edward Watkin's grandiose ideas the cycleway is part of the National Cycle Network Route 6, which runs from Dover to Inverness.

THE BASICS

Distance: 3 miles / 4.8km

Gradient: Steps and slight slopes

Severity: Easy

Approx. time to walk: 1¼ hours

Stiles: None

Maps: OS Landranger 140 (Leicester); Explorer 233 (Leicester & Hinckley)

Path description: Tarmac cycleway, good paths and substantial riverbank

Start point: Riverside Park, car park off Aylestone Road, Leicester (GR SK 578018)

Parking: Riverside Park off Aylestone Road (LE2 8TB)

Dog friendly: Yes

Public toilets: None

Nearest food: Shops and takeaways on Aylestone Road; the Black Horse, Narrow Lane, Aylestone and the Cricketers, Grace Road, Aylestone

1. Go back to the bridge crossed on the way in and turn left (north) along the towpath with the River Soar/Grand Union Canal to the right. Continue between St Mary's Mill Lock and the derelict brick building, over the footbridge across the River Biam to the junction of paths this side of the railway bridge.

2. Turn left, up this narrow path between fences, up the gentle slope with the railway to the right, around a dogleg in the path to a T-junction of paths with the Great Central Way.

3. Take this substantial wide path to the left, for a mile and a quarter (2km) to a substantial iron bridge across Braunstone Lane East, cross and turn right, down the steps to the road. Cross this busy road carefully and turn right along the roadside path to the Aylestone Meadows signpost, then turn left and bear right to the river/canal.

4. Walk along the towpath to the left with the river to the right, back to the car park on the left at Aylestone Mill and the starting point.

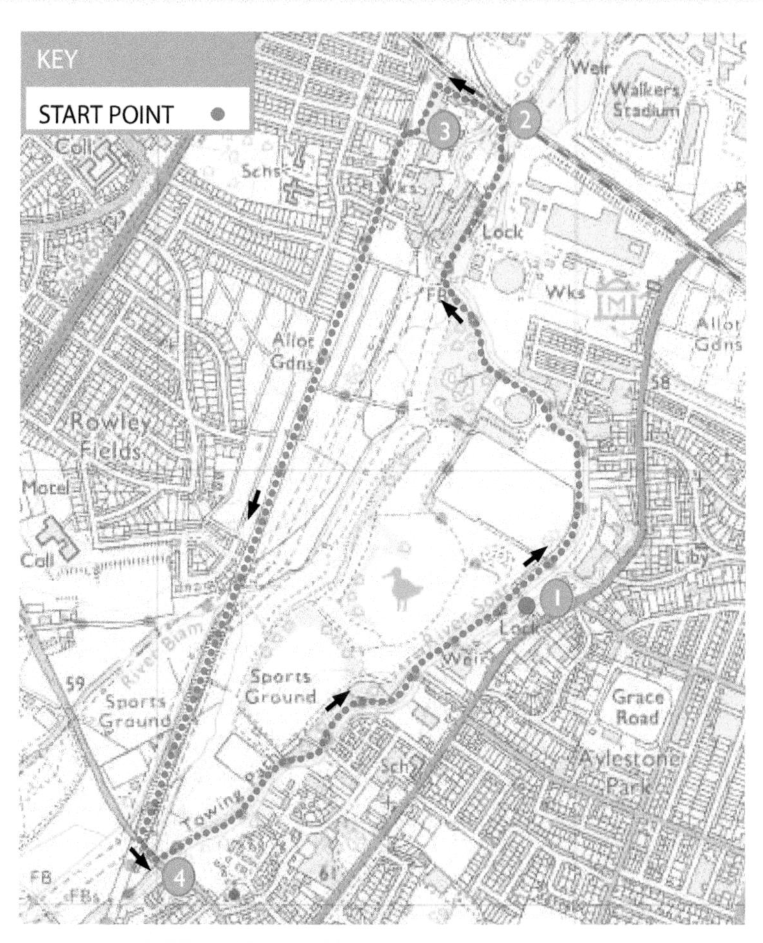
KEY
START POINT
Weir
Walkers Stadium
Schs
Lock
Wks
Allot Gdns
Rowley Fields
Coll
Sports Ground
Towing Path
River Soar
River Biam
Grace Road
Aylestone Park
Lby
FB
1
2
3
4

HOLWELL MINERAL LINE

WHAT APPEARS TO BE A VERY RURAL VILLAGE AND SURROUNDING LANDSCAPE IN FACT HAS A FASCINATING INDUSTRIAL HISTORY.

Ironstone first started to be quarried for building stone in the first part of the 19th century. Many buildings in the area have used ironstone as the basic construction material. When first cut the stone is a grey colour but it soon oxidises into a reddish brown. Looking around the village, it will be noticed that many of the buildings are made from this source. Its value after processing as a source of iron was quickly taken advantage of and the Holwell Iron Works was set up close to Asfordby. The Holwell Mineral Line was built as a quarry line only, to transport iron ore from various quarries north and east of Melton Mowbray, through Holwell to the Iron Works. The line, which was worked by small steam tank engines, was also connected to the nationwide rail system at Asfordby via the Nottingham and Melton line (now the Old Dalby Test Track).

The ore and ironstone found in this country is of fairly low quality. However, producers found that it was economically viable during the Industrial Revolution and particularly during the two World Wars, when there was a danger that that not enough would reach the country due to the U-boat threat.

During the 1950s it became apparent that the industry needed to be using higher grade ore to be able to compete with foreign imports. This had itself to be imported but economics dictated that less and less local material was used. The Holwell Iron Works closed in 1957 and the Mineral Line struggled on with deliveries to the mainline system until its eventual closure in 1964.

At Holwell village a half-mile (1km) length of the line has been transformed into a nature reserve. Two of the quarries local to the village, Brown's Hill Quarry and North Quarry, have also become nature reserves. All three are looked after by the Leicester and Rutland Wildlife Trust.

THE BASICS

Distance: 2½ miles / 4km

Gradient: Slight slopes only

Severity: Easy

Approx. time to walk: 1¼ hours

Stiles: Several

Maps: OS Landranger 129 (Nottingham & Loughborough); Explorer 246 (Loughborough)

Path description: Hardcore farm roads, village roads (not very busy) and field edges

Start point: The parking area opposite Brown's Hill Quarry Nature Reserve, east of Holwell (GR SK 742236)

Parking: The parking area as above (LE14 4SZ)

Dog friendly: Several stiles and three cattle grids, and dogs are not allowed on the nature reserve

Public toilets: None

Nearest food: The Sugar Loaf on the main A606 in Ab Kettleby (1 mile/1.5km away)

1. Take the road into the village, over the cattle grid and the bridge over the dismantled Holwell Mineral Line; continue through the village to the double signpost just before the junction, opposite Hall Farm.

2. Turn left, upslope on this wide stony track between trees; as the track swings right step over the stile ahead. Bear left across this field, over the stile right of the far left corner, carry on to the stile on the left and cross. Keep direction over the stile next to the wide gate and downslope over the stile next to the wide metal gate. Continue along the wide path, over the bridge and back across the dismantled Holwell Mineral Line.

3. Bear left through a wide wooden gate and right, upslope with the fence and the trees to the right, go past the pylon and through the low gate to the yellow top post close to the top of the slope. Bear left along this gravelly farm track and go over the first cattle grid.

4. At the next gateway/cattle grid marked by a yellow top post turn left, along the field edge with the hedge to the right, over the marked stile left of the far right corner. Continue up the wide track between trees and hedges; keep ahead across two stiles next to the gates and on to the road. Turn left, and walk the short distance back to the parking area.

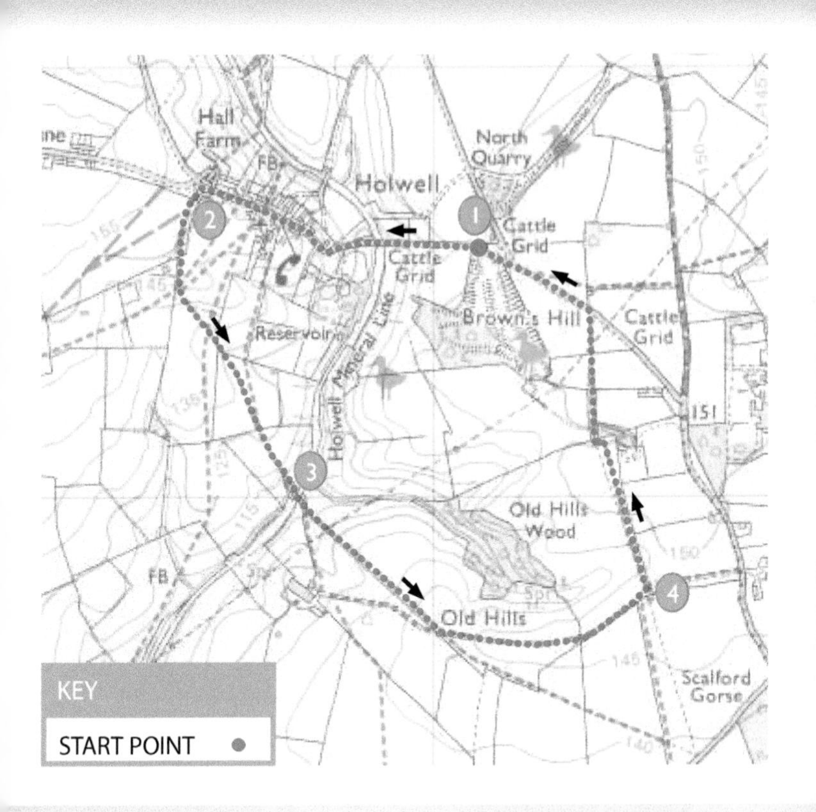
Hall Farm
FB
Holwell
North Quarry
Cattle Grid
Cattle Grid
Brown's Hill
Cattle Grid
Reservoir
Holwell Mineral Line
151
Old Hills Wood
150
FB
Old Hills
145
Scalford Gorse
140
KEY
START POINT

HOLYGATE ROAD

IT IS NORMALLY VERY QUIET IN THIS SECLUDED PART OF THE COUNTRYSIDE UNLESS THERE IS A TRACTOR WORKING CLOSE BY. IN GOOD WEATHER ON THE LAST PART OF THE WALK ALONG THE HIGHER HOLYGATE ROAD, THE SUN MAY BE GLIMPSED REFLECTING ON THE SURFACE OF RUTLAND WATER.

Like the reservoir itself its statistics are impressive. The county of Rutland lost 3 per cent of its total area on its completion. At over four square miles, almost 12 square kilometres, it is the largest lake in England by surface area, holding 124,000 million litres. Kielder Water in Northumberland has a smaller surface area but is deeper and so holds more water. Rutland Water was constructed in the early 1970s and opened in 1975, just in time to help with water shortages during the great drought of 1976. The original intention had been to call the lake Empingham Reservoir; this was changed as the county of Rutland had recently been swallowed by Leicestershire in the reorganisation of counties during 1974.

The dam at the eastern end of the reservoir close to the village of Empingham, crosses the valley of the River Gwash. It is 1300yds/1190m wide and 115ft/35m at the highest point. The River Gwash enters the reservoir close to Manton and continues from an outflow near the dam to keep the river flowing to its confluence with the River Welland between Stamford and Uffington. Levels in the reservoir are kept up by pipelines running from the River Nene near Wansford and the Welland near the Great North Road close to Stamford.

Large numbers of people use the sailing, angling and other leisure facilities that have developed around the lake. A 25-mile/40km track running around the perimeter is popular with cyclists tackling the complete circuit and walkers using a smaller part of it. A boat called the ***Rutland Belle*** sails on a regular voyage around the lake each summer

Wildlife was very quick to adapt the new reservoir for domestic and breeding purposes. A particular success story is the osprey, which was reintroduced into the area in 1996 after birds had been in the area and feeding from fish caught in the lake. The project is very long term but several pairs have been regularly returning and successfully raising young each year of this century.

THE BASICS

Distance: 4 miles / 6.4km

Gradient: One long medium slope on a tarmac surface

Severity: Easy to medium

Approx. time to walk: 2 hours

Stiles: Several stiles but mainly gates

Maps: OS Landranger 141 (Kettering and Corby); Explorer 234 (Rutland Water)

Path description: Grassy fields and tracks; field edges and wider substantial farm roads

Start point: St Mary Magdalene and St Andrew's Church, Main Street, Ridlington (GR SK 847027)

Parking: Sensible roadside parking in the village (LE15 9AU). Limited bus service (check for details)

Dog friendly: Stiles difficult for dogs

Public toilets: None

Nearest food: Nothing in the village; best to go to Uppingham (2 miles/3km)

1. Walk along Main Street, with the church on your left, to the end; go into the driveway ahead and turn immediately right down the wide, hedged track, passing right of the ramparts. Go through the wide metal gate and keep on this track down a slope to the wide metal gate on the left.

2. Turn right, through a narrow gate and left down the field edge; cross the stile and take the path ahead with the barbed-wire fence to the left. Step over the stile and continue ahead on the field edge with the hedge to the left, over the two sleeper footbridge hidden in the hedge just right of the corner.

3. The track continues ahead across the field about 50 yards from the left-hand edge, bearing right to where the hedge juts out. This field may be under cultivation although a track should be well marked within any crop. Keep straight on over the footbridge/stile in the dip at the boundary, and carry on over the stile in the far right corner. Go through the metal gate and keep direction with the River Chater and the ponds to the right, into the corner. Go over the stile and on to the tarmac estate road.

4. Turn left for just over three quarters of a mile (1km) upslope and go between the stone gateposts to the corner.

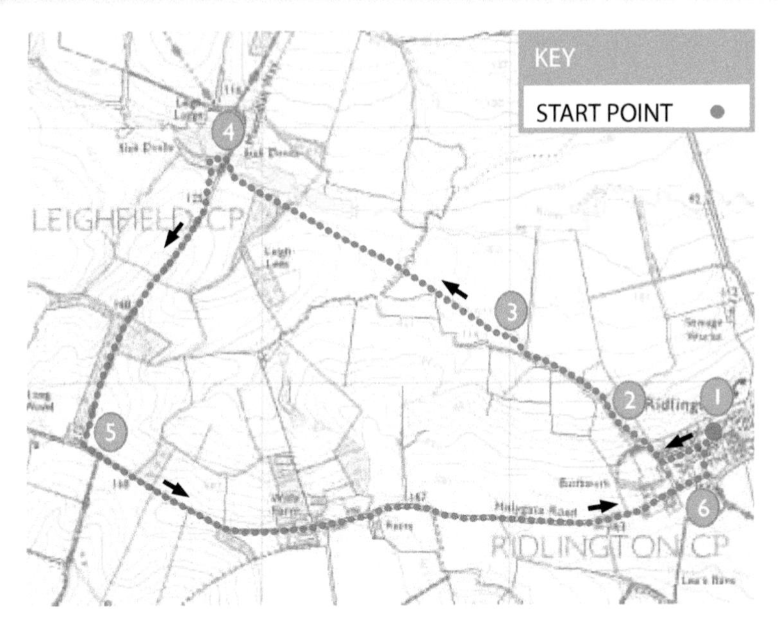

5. Take the stony/gravelly road to the left. Rutland Water can be seen intermittently in the left-hand middle distance. Keep on the road between the farm buildings at Wills Farm and continue along the now tarmac surfaced Holygate Road back to Ridlington village. In this peaceful part of the countryside, the rumble and swish of traffic noise from the A47 trunk road, a mile and a half away at this point, can be heard.

6. Go past the junction with West Lane, right of the high wall to the next junction and turn left along Church Lane to the starting point at the church.

INGARSBY HOLLOW

A DESERTED MEDIEVAL VILLAGE MARKED ONLY BY HUMPS IN THE GROUND AND A GHOSTLY DISUSED AND DISMANTLED RAILWAY LINE. A VIADUCT CAN BE SEEN THROUGH THE TREES AND CLOSE BY IS A MYSTERIOUS SEALED-OFF TUNNEL.

The village of Ingarsby is believed to have been founded in the 9th or 10th century by a Dane called Ingwar; the name is a derivative of 'Ingwar's village'. It was a large settlement at the time of the Domesday Book in 1086 and even in 1352 when the village was given to the Abbey of Leicester there were still twelve families living here.

The Abbey decided in 1469 that they could make more money by enclosing the land and raising sheep and cattle. The villagers were thrown off the land and the village was destroyed. All that remains of the site now are the hummocks on the hillside between points 2 and 3; the humps marking the location of houses and farm buildings and the long shallow channels were village roads.

Ingarsby Old Hall was built after the estate was acquired by the Cave family at the Reformation. The house was mainly built in the 1540s; further building took place during the 1620s.

The railway is the line that used to run from the station at Leicester Belgrave Road to the triangular junction near John o' Gaunt. Trains then ran north to Melton Mowbray and Grantham, or south to Market Harborough and Peterborough. Most passenger services ended in 1953, but goods services continued until 1964. The railway had always carried a lot of holiday and excursion traffic to the east coast seaside resorts and these ran each weekend in summer until the final closure. A tunnel just over a quarter of a mile (0.5km) long was part of the railway between Thurnby and Ingarsby; Covert Lane takes the walker across the top of this tunnel. Massive iron gates have been fitted at one end to keep people out, while at the other end the approaching cutting has been filled with rubbish and the tunnel has been blocked by having sticky clay poured into it.

THE BASICS

Distance: 4¼ miles / 6.8km

Gradient: Moderate slopes up and down throughout

Severity: Moderate

Approx. time to walk: 2½ hours

Stiles: Several

Maps: OS Landranger 141 (Kettering & Corby); Explorer 233 (Leicester & Hinckley)

Path description: Hardcore farm roads, grassy fields and field edges

Start point: Covert Lane, Scraptoft (GR SP 664054)

Parking: Covert Lane near the junction for the farm; beware of farm vehicles (LE7 9SQ)

Dog friendly: Several stiles, not easy for dogs

Public toilets: None

Nearest food: The White House close by in Scraptoft

1. Take the tarmac road further east (away from Scraptoft) and continue in this direction on the wide dirt track to the wide metal gate. Go through and bear left along the wide farm road, continue through the gateway at the end and carry on ahead, passing right of the tumuli known as Monk's Grave, straight on down to the road.

2. Turn left the short distance to the signpost on the right, cross the stile and go up the grassy slope to the track at the top. Turn left – Ingarsby Hollow is down to the left – to the gate and on to the road. Turn right, past the front of Ingarsby Old Hall to the signpost on the left.

3. Step over the stile and keep ahead passing left of the barn to the marker post, then turn right past the end of the barn and through the gate, on to the track of a dismantled railway. Turn left at the marker post down the narrow path between trees, over the stile and down to the fence ahead.

4. Turn left along the field edge with the fence to the right to the marker post, cross the footbridge and go up the slope the other side. Turn left with the stream and the trees now to the left. At the corner, go down the steps by the easily missed yellow top post and cross the stile. Continue with the stream still left to the farm track at the next corner. Turn right, upslope and left over the double stile, along the narrow path through the undergrowth and the stile at the end into a grass field; keep direction passing right of the buildings.

5. At the end, turn right, over two stiles, and keep ahead upslope through several gates marked by yellow top posts. Cross the driveway and the stile the other side. Bear right up this field and over the stile at the top; bear left to the marker post right of the power line post and turn right along the enclosed path between the fence and the hedge. Turn left and bear left to the driveway, take the drive right, through the gate and along the road past the church and the Dog and Gun pub to the T-junction.

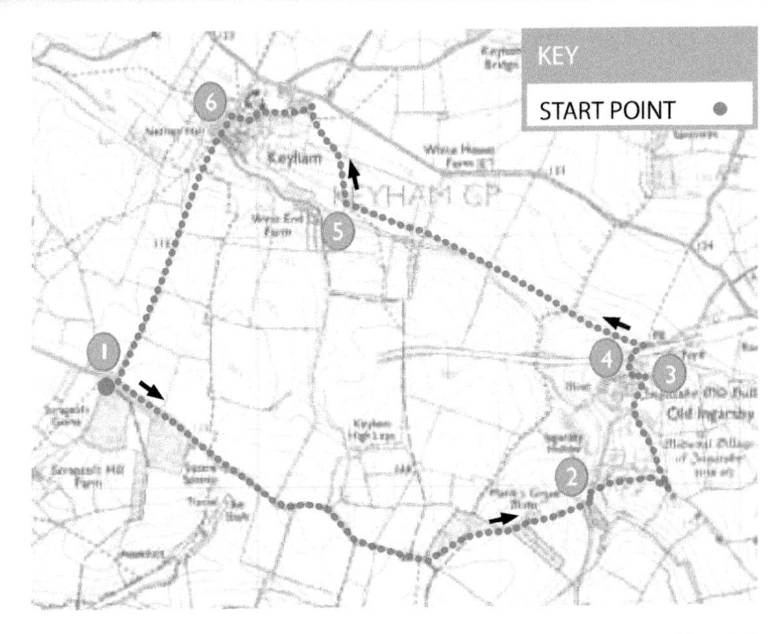

6. Turn left to the stile at the signpost, step over this and the next stile and bear left to the left-hand stile at the yellow top post. Cross the footbridge and bear right then left uphill on the field edge with the hedge to the right. Go over the footbridge right and turn left back upslope with the hedge now left, all the way to the road at the trees and the starting point.

THE LEICESTER AND SWANNINGTON RAILWAY HAS BEEN DISCUSSED ALREADY AT THE START OF THE BAGWORTH INCLINE WALK (NO. 2); PARTS OF THE RAILWAY IN SWANNINGTON ARE LOOKED AFTER BY THE SWANNINGTON HERITAGE TRUST ALONG WITH OTHER SURVIVING SITES FROM THE INDUSTRIAL REVOLUTION SURVIVING LOCALLY.

The Heritage Trust has placed a railway line from the road to the top of the incline, where the sharp slope of the descent may be seen. The incline at Swannington, at 1 in 17, was the steeper of the two inclines on the railway. The slope at Bagworth needed only gravity to let loaded wagons down the slope as they were full going down and pulled empties back up. At Swannington it was the other way round: the wagons were full at the bottom so needed to be pulled up by a cable wound by a steam engine. The brick footings at the top of the incline mark the outline of the engine house and two cottages.

A series of horse-drawn wagonways brought loaded wagons to the bottom of the incline; the engine could bring up three loaded wagons or let down six empty ones. The Leicester and Swannington Railway was taken over by the Midland Railway, who built a diversion to allow trains to avoid the incline, but the stationary engine system continued until the mines it served were closed in 1870. Ironically a steam engine and pump had to be installed at the bottom of the slope and the incline was used to supply coal to the pump engine down the slope in a reversal of its original purpose. This arrangement continued until electric pumps were set up in 1947 and the incline finally closed. The machinery was all dismantled in 1952 and sold for scrap, but the engine from the top of the slope was preserved and can be seen in the National Railway Museum in York.

The cuttings around the two bridges at Church Lane and Potato Lane had suffered from mining subsidence and were filled with mining shale as a safety measure. Only 35 years later the cuttings were excavated and the bridges rebuilt by the Heritage Group and a bridge further down the incline was reinstated.

The railway did not at first cater for passengers, but very quickly introduced some carriages when they realised there was a demand for people to be carried to and from Leicester. These vehicles were for a long time just attached to a normal freight train with no particular timetable to adhere to.

Hough Mill was built in the early years of the 19th century and purchased by John Hough in 1877. The mill had a working life of only about a century and then descended gradually into ruins. When taken over by the Trust it was little more than brick walls, rusting ironwork and badly rotted beams. The Trust has spent a great deal of time and money to stop the mill from falling further into disrepair and has renovated and rebuilt the fabric of the building. Some machinery has been reinstalled and a new cap put into position. The mill is open most Sundays during the summer.

The metal statues of a horse and its driver, close to the replica of a wooden gin in the Gorse Field, recall the primitive method of mechanically hauling coal and miners up from the shallow seams of coal, utilised before the steam power of the Industrial Revolution. Coal has been mined in this locality for over 800 years.

THE BASICS

Distance: 3 miles / 4.8km

Gradient: Easy slopes up and down throughout

Severity: Easy

Approx. time to walk: 1½ hours

Stiles: Several

Maps: OS Landranger 129 (Nottingham & Loughborough); Explorer 245 (The National Forest)

Path description: Hardcore farm roads, grassy fields and field edges. One short stretch may be under cultivation so may be muddy

Start point: The Robin Hood Pub, Spring Lane, Swannington (GR SK 414160)

Parking: Spring Lane or, if you plan to eat there, The Robin Hood pub (LE67 8QQ). Bus service (check details)

Dog friendly: Several stiles, not easy for dogs

Public toilets: None

Nearest food: The Robin Hood as above, also the Station Inn, Hough Hill, Swannington

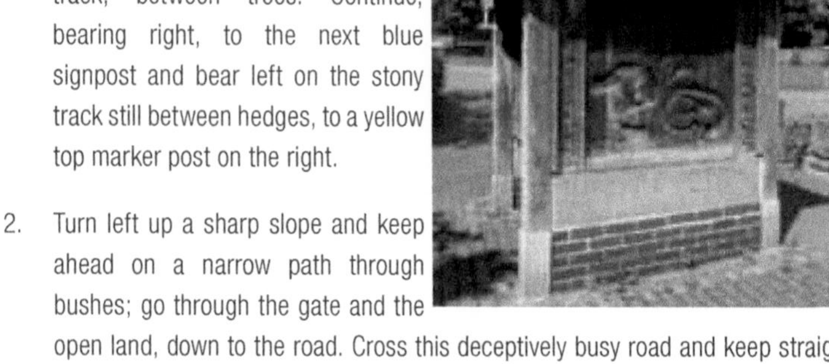

1. Go down the narrow roadway right of the Robin Hood to the blue and green signposts and bear left upslope on this tarmac driveway which soon gives way to a less substantial stony track, between trees. Continue, bearing right, to the next blue signpost and bear left on the stony track still between hedges, to a yellow top marker post on the right.

2. Turn left up a sharp slope and keep ahead on a narrow path through bushes; go through the gate and the open land, down to the road. Cross this deceptively busy road and keep straight on with the railway track to the right, past the brick footings of the engine house. The track descends the Swannington Incline in a cutting with trees either side, under the wooden footbridge at Potato Lane and the rebuilt sandstone and brick bridge at Church Lane.

3. At the signpost just the other side of the bridge turn left across the field ahead, which may be under cultivation although a path should be well marked, to the road. Keep direction on the road right/ahead to Main Street.

4. Take the roadside path to the right, straight over the Limby Hall–Whitwick crossroads, to the footpath signpost on the left. Cross the stile by the gate and bear left to the far left corner, into the trees and follow the path left, through a narrow metal gate and turn left through an adjacent narrow metal gate. Keep on this wide stony track with the horse and its driver figures and the winding gear to the right, to the junction at a yellow top post. Turn right, through the kissing gate into the grounds of Hough Mill.

5. Turn immediate left, through a narrow wooden gate, down a narrow path between hedges to the yellow top marker post just before the house on the right. Turn left, down the left-hand field edge and over the midway stile; carry on to the road.

6. Cross and keep ahead on the left-hand field edge over the stile on the left, bear right over the next marked stile and walk upslope on the path between the hedge and the fence. Step over the stile at the top. Turn right, on the tarmac driveway to the crossroads of drives and turn left down to Main Street (close to point 4). Turn right, down to the junction close to the Robin Hood and the starting point.

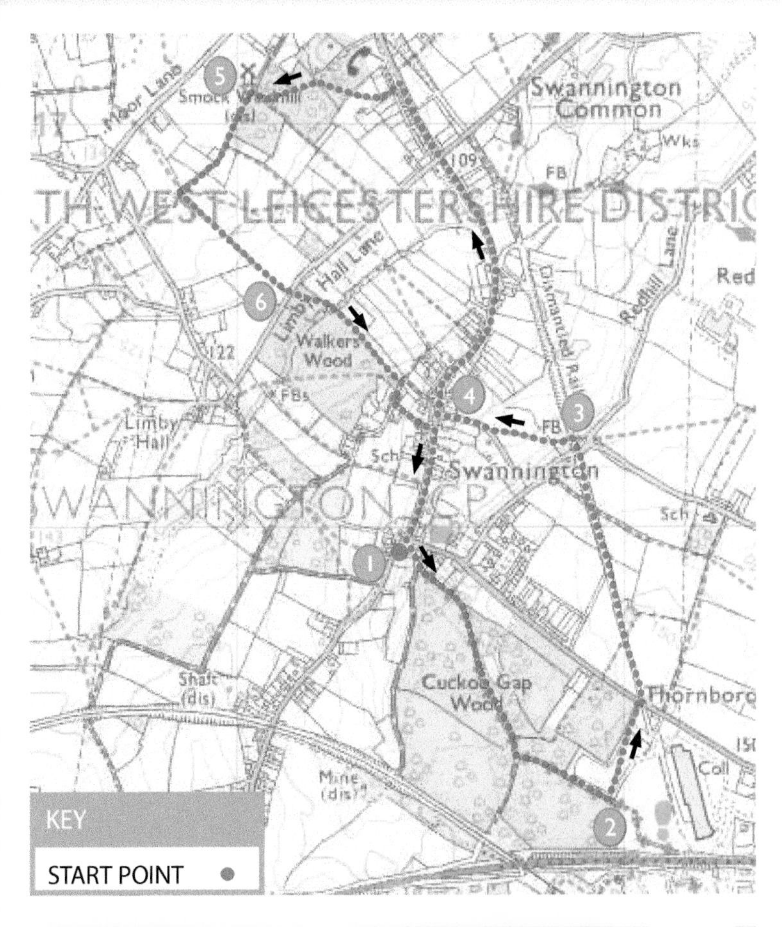
Moor Lane
5
Smock
Swannington
Common
Wks
109
FB
TH WEST LEICESTERSHIRE DISTRIC
Hall Lane
Limby
Dismantled Rai
Redhill Lane
Red
6
Walkers
Wood
122
FBs
4
3
FB
Limby
Hall
Sch
Swannington
WANNINGTON CP
Sch
1
Shaft
(dis)
Cuckoo Gap
Wood
Thornboro
150
Coll
Mine
(dis)
2
KEY
START POINT

Moira Furnace was built to take advantage of the plentiful local supplies of coal and iron ore and the Ashby-de-la-Zouch Canal to take away the finished product.

The furnace was built in 1804 by the Earl of Moira but was not used until 1806. It was never very successful in operation, with everyone blaming everyone else at the time for its failure. Modern technology has revealed that it probably ran too hot with not very high-grade ore. The furnace worked only until 1811. The operators realised that its last load would not be of very good quality and it was still there years later. Ironically the fact that it never worked properly is the main reason it has survived. Had it been successful it would have been adapted, improved and rebuilt in line with developing technology. An adjacent foundry, which was later demolished, operated successfully for many years using pig iron transported on to the site. Other buildings at Moira survived because they were rebuilt into houses. The old engine house built to provide the blast into the furnace now contains a museum.

The towpath of the Ashby-de-la-Zouch Canal (further south) is also part of the Bosworth Field Walk (No. 4). The canal, after a lengthy period of gestation, opened in 1804. It runs from a junction on the Coventry Canal close to Bedworth. The route was originally 31 miles (50km) to Moira, just to the south of Ashby-de-la-Zouch. Several parts of the canal

south of Moira were closed during the mid-20th century because of mining subsidence. Twenty-two miles of canal have always remained open and enthusiasts are now working to restore the rest of the waterway, partly through a new route. A section at Moira Furnace has already been reopened. The canal as originally built was on the level and had no locks; in 2001 a lock had to be constructed close to the end of the canal to allow access to Bath Yard Basin as the land there had subsided.

The path along the dismantled railway is the trackbed of the Ashby and Nuneaton Joint Railway, opened in 1873. Initially a very busy line, passenger services declined quickly after the First World War and were stopped altogether in 1931. Freight services lingered on until total closure in 1971.

The line further south between Shackerstone and Shenton has since been reopened as a heritage railway, known as the Battlefield Line.

THE BASICS

Distance: 3¼ miles / 5.3km

Gradient: Easy

Severity: Easy

Approx. time to walk: 1½ hours

Stiles: None, gates only

Maps: OS Landranger 128 (Derby & Burton upon Trent); Explorer 245 (The National Forest)

Path description: Canal towpaths, good paths and cycleway on dismantled railway track

Start point: Car park on Moira Road, Donisthorpe (GR SK 320143)

Parking: Car park on Moira Road (DE12 7QD). For bus service check details locally.

Dog friendly: Suitable for dogs

Public toilets: None

Nearest food: Pubs, shops and other opportunities in the village

MOIRA FURNACE WALK

1. Leave the car park up the ramp at the rear, walk around the canal basin which is the present end of the Ashby-de-la-Zouch Canal and walk along the towpath with the canal to the right. Carry on past Moira Furnace and the three-gated Moira Lock.

2 Cross this busy road carefully and continue on the towpath with the canal still right, under the striking Marquis Bridge to the fence of 'Conkers' at the far left corner of Bath Yard Basin. Take the path ahead with the fence right and turn left through the gap for the narrow-gauge railway, past the stone Ennstone Trail marker. Follow this track under a bridge beneath a disused railway line.

3. The route leads around, through more open land to a signpost and map board; keep on this trail to the left, leading to a junction of tracks where there is another Ennstone Trail stone marker.

4. Turn left on this substantial path, which is the route of a dismantled railway, for nearly a mile. Go past the Donisthorpe Colliery sign and carry on with the trees on a bank sloping up to the left, to a junction of paths. Turn right, over the brick bridge and immediate left, over a junction of paths to the second junction.

5. Take this path left, round and down across the brick bridge. Keep straight on, curving left back to the canal. Turn right, around the canal basin and down to the car park and the starting point.

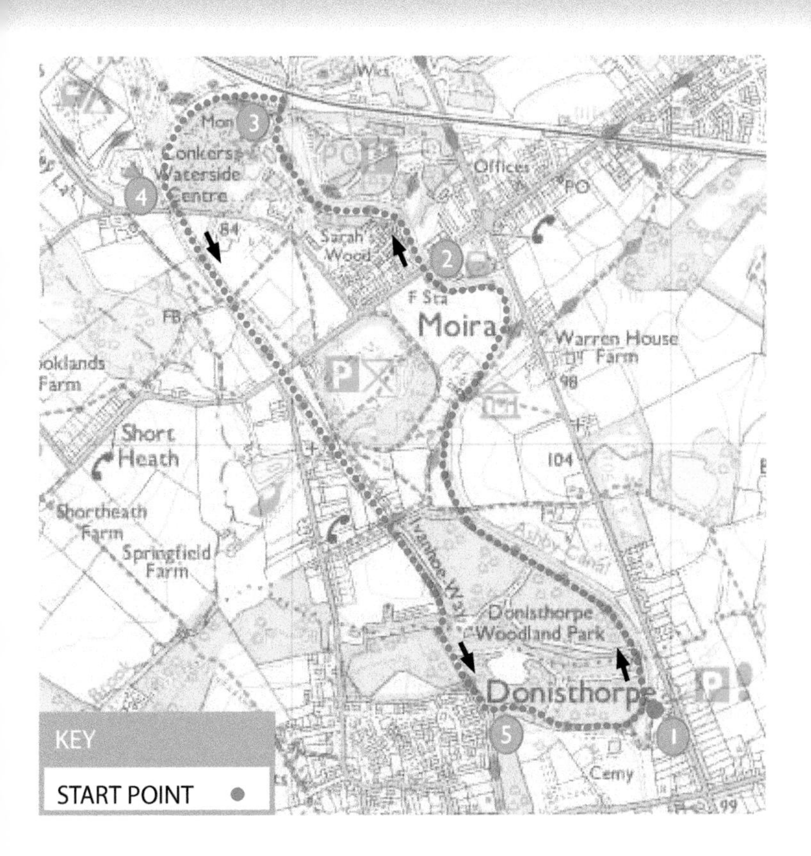
Conkers Waterside Centre
Sarah Wood
Offices
PO
F Sta
Moira
Warren House Farm
Short Heath
Shortheath Farm
Springfield Farm
Ivanhoe Way
Ashby Canal
Donisthorpe Woodland Park
Donisthorpe
Cemy
KEY
START POINT

Tube trains in Leicestershire?

London Transport rolling stock built at Bombardier in Derby is regularly tested on the Old Dalby Test Track and can be seen from this walk. Most brand new electric locos and multiple units are tested here before they enter service on a normal railway line.

The railway was the line from Melton Mowbray to Nottingham which opened in 1880 and closed in 1968; it is 13½ miles/22km long. The area was taken over by the army for the whole of the Second World War and a lot of buildings were erected. These buildings survive as the Crown Business Centre and the fifties married quarters have been sold off to become Queensway Old Dalby.

In 1970 most of the line was reopened as a special track to test the APT-E tilting train that was then in development. The Advanced Passenger Train or APT should have been an outstanding success, but the revolutionary idea that the train tilted at speed rather than the track being banked was beset with problems from the start. A whole series of sometimes minor, but often catastrophic problems took up a great deal of space in newspapers and television news. One of the most damning problems occurred during a press demonstration run when reporters suffered from motion sickness. British Rail did not help when they said that the newspapermen were suffering from the effects of too much liquid hospitality. On a separate demonstration one of the trains stuck in a tilted position, and brakes were a constant difficulty throughout the whole programme. The enthusiasm of management and politicians faded and the project came to an end during the mid-1980s. An interesting footnote is that an APT unit travelling on the Old Dalby line reached 143mph/231kph in January 1976; another unit held the British Rail speed record of 162mph/261kph between 1979 and 2002.

The idea and expertise were sold to Fiat and have been successfully adopted by several other manufacturers. In the early years of this century the track was used to test the new Virgin 'Pendolino' trains currently used on the West Coast Main Line, which use the same technology. A new generation of tilting trains, the 'Hitachi Super Express', which are due to be introduced during 2017/18 on the East Coast and Great Western Main Lines, will also be tested at Old Dalby.

THE BASICS

Distance: 3 ¾ miles / 6km

Gradient: Easy to moderate slopes up and down throughout

Severity: Easy to moderate

Approx. time to walk: 2 hours

Stiles: Several

Maps: OS Landranger 129 (Nottingham & Loughborough); Explorer 246 (Loughborough)

Path description: Hardcore farm roads, grassy fields, woodland paths and field edges. Some fields are also crossed which may be under cultivation so could be muddy

Start point: St John the Baptist Church, Church Lane, Old Dalby (GR SK 673237)

Parking: Roadside parking space in the village (LE14 3LB). For bus services check local details

Dog friendly: Several stiles, not easy for dogs

Public toilets: None

Nearest food: The Crown Inn, Debdale Hill, Old Dalby

1. Facing away from the church turn right, and go past the wooden steps and the first footpath signpost, to the second signpost on the right. Go through the gate and follow the path left over the stream, then right over the footbridge and stile. Carry on up the field edge into the corner, turn left to the yellow topped marker post and go through the wide gap.

2. Bear left, across the field which may be under cultivation, although a path may be well marked; it is often easier here to walk left into the corner and turn right, along the field edges to the marker posts. Cross the stile and the next two fields, where tracks should be visible within any crops, over the midway stile to the far stile.

3. Step over and follow the path through the undergrowth above the tunnel. Keep straight on through trees to the stile and cross. Bear right, over a footbridge at a marker post to the corner of the trees; bear left and follow the path right, past a pond. Bear right, over a footbridge with handrails and turn left upslope, past a marker post with the trees to the left over the stile at the wide metal gate. Keep left to another wide metal gate.

4. Turn right, along the field edge with the trees left bearing right to the marker post at the far right next to the double power line poles. Go over the stile and up the path to the road. Cross this surprisingly busy road carefully and turn left to the signpost on the right.

5. Take the wide drive passing right of the green barn, over the stile at the gate and bear right, through the narrow gate. The route now passes over the top of the Grimston Tunnel for which there is a ventilation shaft down to the left. Continue ahead through the gateway and bear left at the yellow top post. Go past the marker post in the midway dip and keep direction over stiles marked by yellow-topped marker posts all the way to the wide metal gate at the road in Grimston village.

6. Go through and turn right along the roadside path, through the churchyard, left of the church to the concrete steps on the right. Go up and follow the path, between walls, through the roofed section (mind your heads!) and around corners to the stile. Step over and turn left, down this long field, over the double stile at the far end. Bear left through a wide metal gate and turn right, back to the original direction with the hedge to the right, over the stile and carry on to the road.

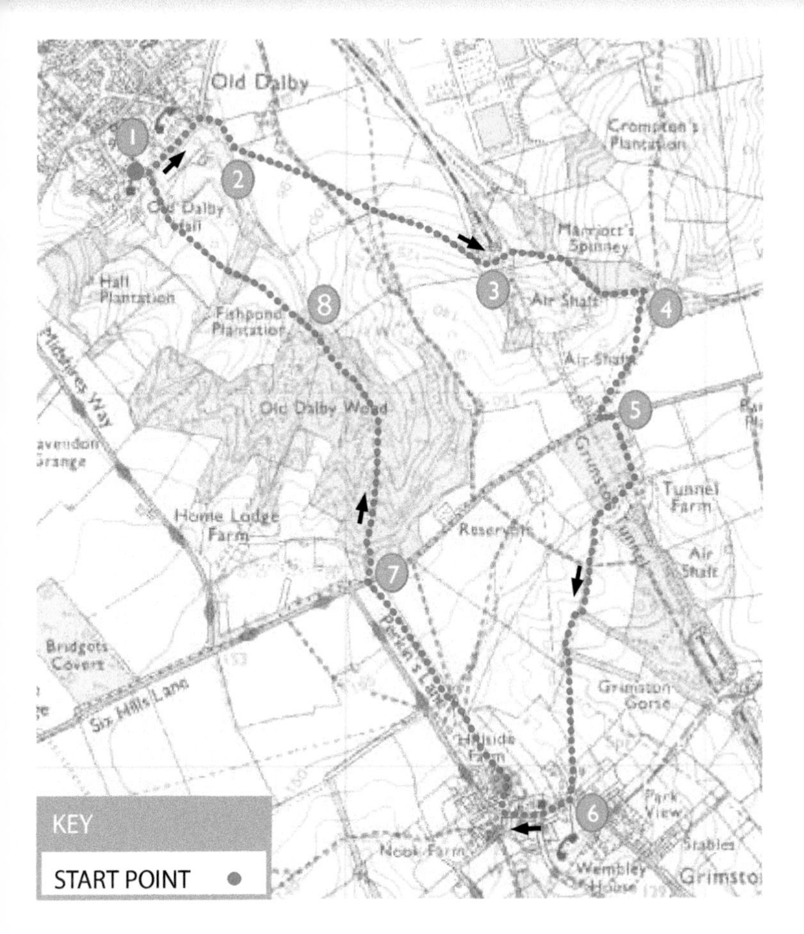

7. Cross carefully back over the road and keep ahead, through the gate and down the wide track through the trees of Old Dalby Wood. Bear right at the marker post at the fork and then follow the path back down to rejoin the wider track. Continue upslope to a yellow top marker post and turn right along the path, downhill and over what may be a very slippery narrow footbridge. Carry on through a gate and out of the trees.

8. Keep direction over another narrow footbridge and a field which may be under cultivation, over the next stile and down the path through the narrow belt of trees. Bear right across this grassy field to the stile at the yellow top post right of the ha-ha in front of Old Dalby Hall. Cross and carry on to the road, turn left back to the church.

Bradgate Park was the ancestral home of one of the most tragic figures in English history, Lady Jane Grey, who is thought to have been born here in about 1537.

An apocryphal tale tells of Old John Tower being built as a memorial to an aged retainer who had died in a bonfire accident during a birthday celebration. A more likely explanation is that it is just another 18th-century folly.

Thomas Grey built Bradgate House in the early years of the 16th century; it is thought that the house was finished by 1520. The estate, forfeited to the crown in 1554, was returned in 1563. The Greys, who became Earls of Stamford in 1628, did not use Bradgate as a residence from the early 18th century; it was retained only as a sporting estate for shooting and game. It continued to be their property until 1928 when it was offered to the city of Leicester for public use, but unfortunately the purchase price could not be found.

Sir Charles Bennion (1857–1929) was a local businessman and philanthropist who started to build shoe manufacturing equipment in Leicester in the 1880s. The company became part of British United Shoe Manufacturing, of which he was Managing Director from 1899 to 1929. Bennion bought the park and presented it to 'the city and county of Leicester that for all time it might be preserved in its natural state for the quiet enjoyment of the people of Leicestershire'.

The estate had been held during the medieval period by the Ferrers of Groby, and it passed to the Grey family in 1445 when the 6th Baroness Ferrers married Edward Grey. In the convoluted world of politics and marriage in the 15th and 16th centuries, their son Sir John Grey was the first husband of Elizabeth Woodville, who became the Queen of Edward IV. Sir John was a Lancastrian supporter in the Wars of the Roses and died at the Second Battle of St Albans in 1461. His great grandson born in 1517 was Henry Grey, who married Lady Frances Brandon, granddaughter of Henry VII by his daughter Mary Tudor. Lady Frances and her descendants therefore had a place in the line of succession to the English throne.

Henry Grey schemed with Edward's Lord Protector and Regent the Duke of Somerset, trying to get his daughter Jane married to the sickly teenage king. The plan failed and although Henry got off scot free, the Duke of Northumberland took the opportunity to overthrow Somerset and take the Regency himself. Somerset was convicted of trumped-up charges of treason and beheaded.

As the health of the king deteriorated Northumberland looked for a way to retain power, and arranged for his son Lord Guildford Dudley to marry Lady Jane. Edward already believed his two elder sisters Mary and Elizabeth to be illegitimate as his father had annulled both marriages; Northumberland gained his agreement to name Jane as his successor.

Edward died on 6 July 1553 and Jane was declared Queen on the 9th; she is reputed to have accepted the crown reluctantly and although it was traditional for English monarchs to reside in the Tower until they were crowned, Northumberland kept her there, locked up.

Mary immediately began to rally support around her Hertfordshire residence and Northumberland set out with a small army to capture her. As soon as he had left London, however, the Privy Council and Parliament changed sides, declaring Mary to be Queen on 19 July, to the delight of the citizens of London. Northumberland was beheaded on 22 August; Jane, her husband and her father were initially spared.

In early 1554, however, there was a revolt by people in Kent led by Thomas Wyatt against Mary and her plans to marry Prince Philip, the Spanish prince who later became King Philip II. The rebel army led by Wyatt entered London but was easily defeated and the rebellion put down. Jane's father had joined the rebels and Mary now acknowledged the threat of Jane's presence as the figurehead of a future uprising. Jane and her husband were beheaded on 12 February and her father on the 23rd February.

THE BASICS

Distance: 3½ miles / 5.6km

Gradient: One moderate slope up and the same down

Severity: Easy to moderate

Approx. time to walk: 1¾ hours

Stiles: None

Maps: OS Landranger 129 (Nottingham & Loughborough, 140 Leicester); Explorer 246 (Loughborough)

Path description: Rough tracks and slopes, good paths

Start point: Hallgates car park at the north-west corner of Cropston Reservoir (GR SK 542114)

Parking: Car park as above (LE7 7HQ). Bus service available (check details)

Dog friendly: Good for dogs

Public toilets: In the car park

Nearest food: Deer Barn Tea Room, three-quarters of the way round the route. Also the Bradgate Arms and the Badgers Sett, pubs in Cropston village

OLD JOHN TOWER WALK

1. Go through the high kissing gate in the wall at the back of the car park and turn right along the track with the wall to the right, through the gateway at the end. Fork right, upslope with the wall and the trees of Hallgate Hill Spinney to the right, bearing gently left to the information board at Hunt's Hill.

2. Turn left, up the steeper slope to Old John Tower and continue down the steep slope the other side, bearing right close to the trees. Take the path then bearing left and right, passing close to the left-hand edge of Bowling Green Spinney.

3. Go through the gap in the wall and down the path with the wall to the left, past the ruins of Bradgate Hall to the narrow tarmac road.

4. Turn left; follow this road past the toilets and tearoom all the way back to the kissing gate and the Hallgates car park.

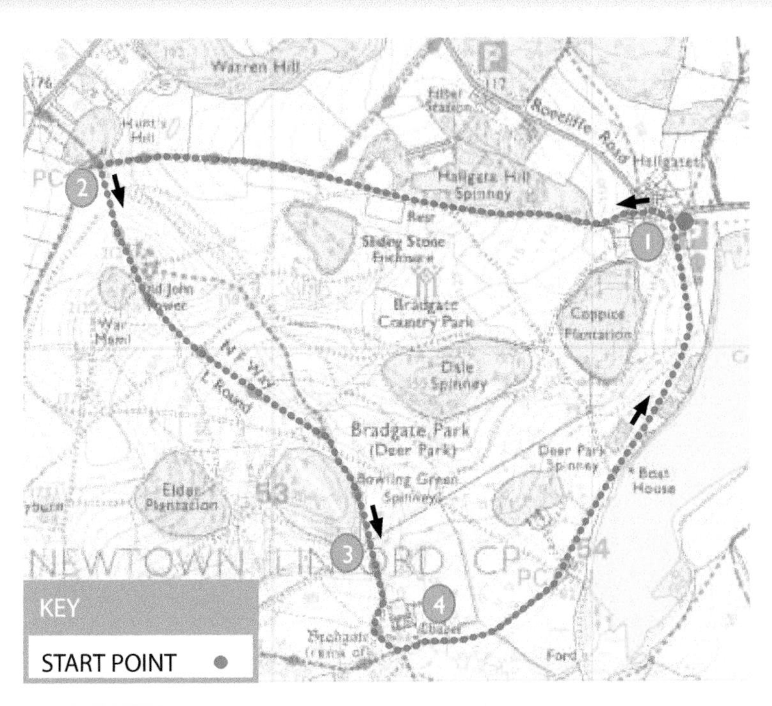
Warren Hill
Hunt's Hill
Roecliffe Road
Hallgates
Hallgate Hill Spinney
Sliding Stone Enclosure
Bradgate Country Park
Old John Tower
War Meml
Coppice Plantation
Dale Spinney
NF Way
L Round
Bradgate Park
(Deer Park)
Bowling Green Spinney
Deer Park Spinney
Boat House
Elder Plantation
NEWTOWN LINFORD CP
Chapel
Bradgate (ruins of)
Ford
KEY
START POINT

IN RECENT TIMES FOXTON LOCKS HAS BECOME A BUSY TOURIST DESTINATION. UNTIL THE RECENT BOOM IN LEISURE BOATING ON CANALS, HOWEVER, IT WAS VERY MUCH A WORKING SITE.

There are two flights of staircase locks; a staircase lock is where the top gate of a lock is the bottom gate of the next lock on the way up. The whole area becomes very crowded in busy holidays; the canals with boats, the towpaths with onlookers eating ice creams and the pubs with people sitting enjoying the ambience.

The modern leisure narrowboat enthusiast is finding at Foxton the same problem that working boats had through the 19th and the first half of the 20th centuries. The locks are a bottleneck, with far too many boats waiting to use them at busy times.

The Grand Union Canal has quite a convoluted history. The River Soar north of Leicester was converted into a canal or 'navigation' in 1794. Investors in the Leicester and Nottingham area quickly saw the possibility of constructing a canal from the River Soar to connect with the Grand Junction Canal at Northampton. This canal, the Leicestershire and Northamptonshire Union Canal, authorised in 1793, was quickly opened to Debdale Wharf near Kibworth, but always struggled financially and had only reached Market Harborough by 1810. Another company called the Grand Union was formed to connect the canal from Foxton to Norton Junction (the nearest convenient point). The canal had two tunnels, one at Crick and the second at Husbands Bosworth; these were both built wide enough for boats to pass within them, whereas all the locks were built to take only one boat at a time. The Grand Union was also never very financially secure as it depended on tolls for passing traffic rather than the full tariff for the complete journey.

Competition from the railways reduced business even more but the canals struggled on until 1894, when both were bought by the Grand Junction and became that company's Leicester Line. The new company took the name Grand Union later in 1929 and the original is now referred to as the 'Old Grand Union'.

The new company realised that Foxton and the other staircase locks at Watford were a big problem and resolved to do something about it. Between 1898 and 1900 an inclined plane was built close to the locks. The plane has two tanks or caissons that it hauled up and down a slope with steam power. In an ideal situation two boats entered the caissons at the bottom and two at the top. The balance between the two was adjusted with more water so that the top weighed slightly more than the bottom. Very little effort was then required to transfer boats both ways.

There were two immediate benefits: the journey time for boats through Foxton was reduced from 45 minutes or an hour down to 12 minutes; the loss of water through the system was also negligible as the same amount of water lost in the descending caisson was replaced by the one going up. The plane was an immediate success, so much so that a lot of money had to be spent on the locks later because they had deteriorated through lack of use. There was also a downside: wider boats could still not be used because a planned inclined plane was never built at Watford and the cost of keeping steam in the system ready for boats to use as soon as they arrived proved to be prohibitive. The plane was taken out of service in 1911 and sold for scrap in 1928. The remains of the plane can still be seen and a museum has a display of what the plane was like in use.

THE BASICS

Distance: 3¼ miles / 5.2km

Gradient: Two slopes: one easy, one moderate

Severity: Easy

Approx. time to walk: 1¾ hours

Stiles: Several stiles

Maps: OS Landranger 141 (Kettering and Corby); Explorer 223 (Northampton and Market Harborough)

Path description: Canal towpaths, hard paths and field edges

Start point: Foxton Country Park car park, Gumley Road, Foxton (GR SP 691891)

Parking: Foxton Country Park, pay and display (LE16 7RR). Bus service available (check details)

Dog friendly: Stiles make the walk not brilliant for dogs

Public toilets: In the car park

Nearest food: Bridge 61 and Foxton Locks Inn at the Bottom Lock. An ice cream van is usually in the car park on busy weekends

SHOP

1. Take the signposted footpath over the bridge and down to the opposite towpath and walk down the path with the canal and the locks to the right. Cross the footbridge at the Bottom Lock to the right and double back across the canal on Bridge 61, then continue down this wide stony track through the metal gate.

2. Bear right, over to the right-hand hedge, and carry on along the field edge with the hedge to the right up and over the rise and down to the road. Cross this deceptively busy road carefully and go through the field and out through the gate the other side. Turn left along this road for 120 yards to the signpost at the field entrance.

3. Turn right, then immediate left. Take the path on the right with the trees to the right, past the first yellow top marker post. Bear right at the next yellow top post, over the stream and

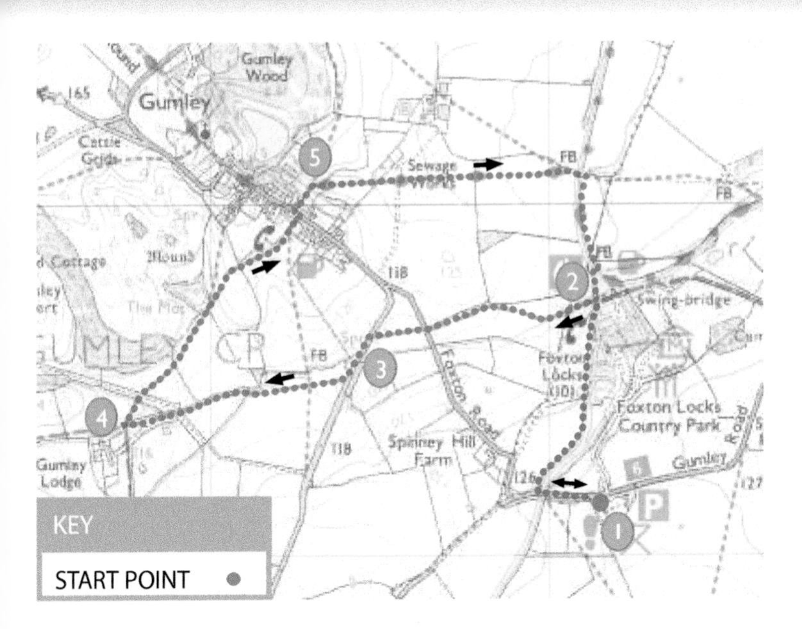

keep on the right-hand edge of this field, with trees still to the right, past the wooden gate in the hedge gap at the end. Go through the next narrow wooden gate and up the tarmac drive for 90 yards, bear right with the hedge and the trees to the right, past the yellow top posts and turn right, through the gate.

4. Bear right, through two narrow metal gates, and carry on through the wide hedge gap at the marker post. Cross over the footbridge and go through the gate at the far left; keep ahead upslope with the fence to the right, through gates and between houses to the road. Turn left and immediate right at the signpost downslope to the marker post and bear right to the kissing gate.

5. Keep in a straight line, through kissing gates all the way to the canal and cross the flimsy-looking narrow footbridge. Turn right, along the towpath with the canal to the right to Rainbow Bridge (No. 62). Cross and take the towpath left, past the buildings and back upslope with the locks to the left. Cross the bridge back to the car park and the starting point.

SADDINGTON TUNNEL

THE HALF-MILE LONG TUNNEL WAS ONE OF THE FIRST OPENED ON ENGLAND'S CANAL SYSTEM. BUILT AND EXCAVATED ENTIRELY WITH HAND TOOLS AND MUSCLE, IT IS VERY SIMPLE IN CONSTRUCTION BUT NEVERTHELESS ONE OF THE WONDERS OF THE EARLY INDUSTRIAL REVOLUTION.

Early canals were cut or built as much as possible on the level; on encountering a slope the civil engineer responsible would often take the canal around the contours to avoid any changes in levels. The canal might also go through a man-made cutting as an expensive option, or, as was found necessary at Saddington, a tunnel could be bored; a very expensive option. If all else failed then locks would have to be built; they were sometimes necessary anyway on gentle or continuous slopes. Locks were a nuisance, as they slowed traffic down and wasted water.

A working canal uses prodigious amounts of water; just one narrowboat can take up to 50,000 gallons of water with it through a lock or system of locks. This water has to be replaced so that following boats can continue to use the waterway.

The working of a canal often depends on it being built with as long a 'summit' section as possible, so that the water it loses every time a lock is used does not have a great effect. The canal needs to have a constant supply to this section; the best method of doing this is to build the canal so that it has a stream or natural source of water flowing directly into it. The canal companies had to pay for this privilege, of course, and the system had its drawbacks as the canal companies often had to agree limits on the amount of water they used or arrange to return the same amount of water further down the watercourse. In Northamptonshire, streams supply the Welford and Sulby reservoirs close to the village of Welford. A branch or arm runs from the reservoir to supply the water needed for the summit section of the Grand Union Canal between Foxton and Watford, next to the M1. This system has the added advantage that the arm can be used as part of the canal. Saddington Reservoir, which was built at the same time as the canal in 1802, keeps the canal water supply at the right level on the lower section north of Foxton Locks.

Mill Field Wood to the right of the canal and north of the tunnel and east of the village was acquired by the Woodland Trust and planted during 2000 by local villagers who refer to it as Millennium Wood. Fleckney has a history as a major producer of bricks through the 19th century. The duck pond in the middle of the village started as a clay pit to supply local manufacturers.

THE BASICS

Distance: 4¼ miles / 6.8km

Gradient: Flat with one easy slope

Severity: Easy

Approx. time to walk: 2 hours

Stiles: Mostly gates but several stiles

Maps: OS Landranger 141 (Kettering and Corby, right on the edge); Explorer 223 (Northampton and Market Harborough) and 233 (Leicester & Hinckley)

Path description: Canal towpaths, hard paths and field edges

Start point: High Street, Fleckney (GR SP 649935)

Parking: Car park on High Street in Fleckney (LE8 8AJ). Check local details for bus services

Dog friendly: Stiles make the walk not brilliant for dogs

Public toilets: None

Nearest food: The Old Crown Inn and the Golden Shield in Fleckney

1. Go out of the car park and over the adjacent zebra crossing, turn right and immediate left along Main Street with the stream to the left for 500 yards to the signpost on the left.

2. Turn left, up the wide tarmac path, over the footbridge, through two kissing gates and up the field edge with the wire fence to the left, through the next kissing gate. Keep direction on the path at the back of the houses and the edge of the playing field. Continue through the wooden kissing gate and, passing left of Fleckney Lodge, follow the track left and right, over a farm drive and through a metal kissing gate. Carry on up the left-hand field edge with the hedge and houses still left, bearing right, to a yellow top marker post in the wide hedge gap.

3. Keep direction right of the pond and go through the two marked gates in the right-hand hedge. Turn left to the yellow top post at the far left and go through the gate to the road, cross and keep ahead up the farm driveway and bear right, through the wooden kissing gate. Carry on along the enclosed path, up this narrow lane to the junction with the road in Saddington village; cross and walk downhill between walls and through the kissing gate.

4. Continue through the kissing gate ahead and up and over the rise, through the next kissing gate and over this rise, down through the kissing gate and over both footbridges.

5. Turn left in front of the footbridge/sluice gate with the embankment to the right. The stream is an artificial channel built from Saddington Reservoir to supply the canal; the embankment was built to keep the supply channel level above the valley created by the Saddington and Laughton brooks. As the channel veers right, cross the footbridge/stile left of the wide metal gate and keep direction with the trees to the left. Bear left, below a yellow top post up on the right, to a yellow top post at the trees and go down the wide track through trees. Bear left over the bridge, with the embankment to the right, up to the aqueduct.

6. Turn right, through the arch and immediate left up the narrow path to the canal. Turn right, along the towpath with the canal to the left, under the road and keep

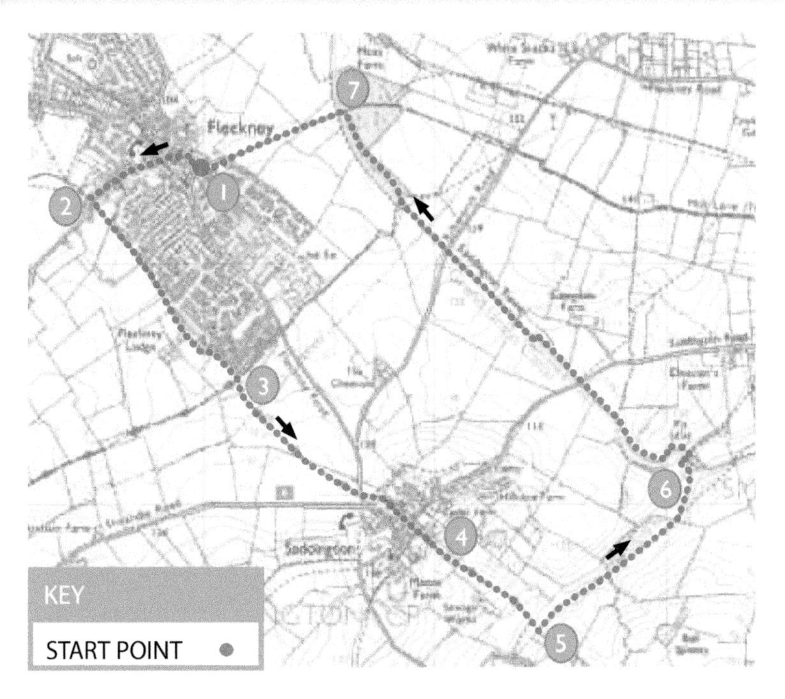

on the path upslope above the tunnel portal. Follow the path ahead between hedges and above the tunnel; continue direction over the road to the yellow top post just before the far portal. Turn right, bearing left along the wide path parallel to, but above the canal, to the marker post at the brick bridge.

7. Cross over the bridge and keep straight on across the ridge and furrow field to the gate, keep ahead along the stony road to the junction. Turn right to the road in Saddington; the car park is 70 yards to the right.

Sheet Hedges Wood is a Site of Special Scientific Interest (SSSI), consisting of three fairly separate parts. The oldest and largest section was mentioned in the Domesday Book (1086).

The part next to the road is newer, where a lot of the trees were planted towards the end of the 20th century. What was once a meadow between the two parts has had five thousand saplings planted and the grassy areas reseeded to encourage native wild flowers and new growth of grass for regular crops of hay.

Groby Pool (the local pronunciation is 'Grooby') has been a SSSI since 1956. There are a wide range of birds and insects, some very common and some not so common, particularly wildfowl, who call the pool home. There had been constant speculation among historians and archaeologists as to whether the pool is a natural rock formation or man-made. Recent research seems to point to aspects of artificial construction. The first mention of the pool is in records dated 1297, which leads to the opinion that it was made by damming Slate Brook in early medieval times; probably under the direction of monks from Leicester Abbey.

A quarry was once in operation between the pool and Groby and a large quarry still operates east of the pool and south of Sheet Hedges Wood, but remains mostly out of sight. A railway once ran between the quarry and Groby along the track of the footpath access, but it has been closed since 1967 and the stone is now all moved by road.

Look out for the old-fashioned police box still in use by the local force in the Bradgate Park car park in Newtown Linford village.

THE BASICS

Distance: 3¼ miles / 5.2km

Gradient: One moderate slope up and the same down

Severity: Easy to moderate

Approx. time to walk: 1¾ hours

Stiles: Mainly gates but some stiles

Maps: OS Landranger 140 (Leicester, right on the edge); Explorer 233 (Leicester and Hinckley)

Path description: Roadside paths, farm roads, grassy fields, woodland paths and short field sections which may be under cultivation and muddy in the wet

Start point: Newtown Linford Lane (GR SK 525079)

Parking: Groby Pool car park (LE6 0FF). Check local information for bus services.

Dog friendly: Some stiles, making it more difficult for dogs

Public toilets: None

Nearest food: The Stamford Arms in Groby village, the Bradgate and the Grey Lady restaurant in Newtown Linford

SHEET HEDGES WOOD WALK

1. Turn right from the car park entrance along the roadside path to the signpost just this side of the A50 access ramp junction. Turn left over the stile and follow the potholed road to the yellow-topped marker post on the left. Turn left up to the footbridge and cross to the right, keep ahead over the farm road and through the kissing gate.

2. Turn left, along the field edge with the trees to the left. Carry on over the footbridge at the end and across the field ahead, upslope, which may be under cultivation although a track should be visible within any crop. At the marker post at the corner of Sheet Hedges Wood, go through the kissing gate and continue upslope with the trees to the left.

3. Go through the kissing gate at the top corner and turn left along the edge of this field with the trees of the wood still left, through the gate and into the trees at the end, bearing left then right, through the next kissing gate. Take a diagonal across the field to the yellow top marker post and carry on to the left with the hedge to the right. A track should be visible although this field may have a crop in it. At the junction of boundaries keep direction ahead on the left-hand edge of the right-hand field; bear right to the marker post near the barn.

4. Step over the stile and turn left along the enclosed path, turn right at the end along the path with the barn to the right and keep direction down to the road. Turn left to the footpath signpost, just this side of the Post Office.

5. Turn left up the enclosed path and continue up the slope of the narrow field and exit over the stile at the yellow top post at the top left, out on to the road.

6. Cross slightly right, through the kissing gate and go down the wide track between the fence and the hedge, through the gate and bear right, downslope. Follow the track left at the marker post and continue through open ground curving left with the track, with trees to the left past a wide metal gate. Follow the narrower path all the way to the road.

7. Take the roadside path to the right, back to the car park and starting point.